At a DESQview menu with fill-in fields:

↵	Completes a menu entry.
Tab	Moves the cursor to the next menu entry.
Shift-Tab	Moves the cursor to the previous menu entry.
Ctrl-End	Erases a field blank from the cursor to the end of the blank.
Home	Moves the cursor to the first field in the window.
End	Moves the cursor to the space following the last character in the field.
Arrow keys	Move the cursor up, down, left, or right within the menu area.
Esc	Cancels the currently displayed menu.
Backspace	Erases backward from the cursor, one character at a time.
Delete	Erases forward from the cursor, one character at a time.
Insert	Toggles the keyboard between insert mode and overwrite mode.

With DESQview Learn:

	Overrides a mapped key and deactivates playback of its script.
Ctrl-Break	Aborts the current script.

Computer users are not all alike.
Neither are SYBEX books.

We know our customers have a variety of needs. They've told us so. And because we've listened, we've developed several distinct types of books to meet the needs of each of our customers. What are you looking for in computer help?

If you're looking for the basics, try the **ABC's** series, or for a more visual approach, select **Teach Yourself**.

Mastering and **Understanding** titles offer you a step-by-step introduction, plus an in-depth examination of intermediate-level features, to use as you progress.

Our **Up & Running** series is designed for computer-literate consumers who want a no-nonsense overview of new programs. Just 20 basic lessons, and you're on your way.

SYBEX **Encyclopedias** provide a *comprehensive reference* and explanation of all of the commands, features and functions of the subject software.

Sometimes a subject requires a special treatment that our standard series doesn't provide. So you'll find we have titles like **Advanced Techniques, Handbooks, Tips & Tricks**, and others that are specifically tailored to satisfy a unique need.

You'll find SYBEX publishes a variety of books on every popular software package. Looking for computer help? Help Yourself to SYBEX.

For a complete catalog of our publications:

SYBEX Inc.

2021 Challenger Drive, Alameda, CA 94501
Tel: (415) 523-8233/(800) 227-2346 Telex: 336311
Fax: (415) 523-2373

SYBEX is committed to using natural resources wisely to preserve and improve our environment. This is why we have been printing the text of books like this one on recycled paper since 1982.

This year our use of recycled paper will result in the saving of more than 15,300 trees. We will lower air pollution effluents by 54,000 pounds, save 6,300,000 gallons of water, and reduce landfill by 2,700 cubic yards.

In choosing a SYBEX book you are not only making a choice for the best in skills and information, you are also choosing to enhance the quality of life for all of us.

DESQview
Instant Reference

DESQview™
Instant Reference

Paul J. Perry

San Francisco • Paris • Düsseldorf • Soest

Acquisitions Editor: Dianne King
Developmental Editor: James A. Compton
Copy Editor: Judith Bellamy
Project Editor: Janna Hecker
Technical Editor: Charles Russel
Word Processors: Scott Campbell and Ann Dunn
Book Designer: Ingrid Owen
Layout: Charlotte Carter
Screen Graphics: Cuong Le
Desktop Publishing Production: Len Gilbert
Proofreader: Bill Cassel
Indexer: Tom McFadden
Cover Designer: Archer Design
Screen reproductions produced by XenoFont.

DESQview, DESQview 386, QEMM-386, and Manifest are trademarks of Quarterdeck Office Systems.

XenoFont is a trademark of XenoSoft.

SYBEX is a registered trademark of SYBEX, Inc.

TRADEMARKS: SYBEX has attempted throughout this book to distinguish proprietary trademarks from descriptive terms by following the capitalization style used by the manufacturer.

SYBEX is not affiliated with any manufacturer.

Every effort has been made to supply complete and accurate information. However, SYBEX assumes no responsibility for its use, nor for any infringement of the intellectual property rights of third parties which would result from such use.

Copyright ©1991 SYBEX Inc., 2021 Challenger Drive, Alameda, CA 94501. World rights reserved. No part of this publication may be stored in a retrieval system, transmitted, or reproduced in any way, including but not limited to photocopy, photograph, magnetic or other record, without the prior agreement and written permission of the publisher.

Library of Congress Card Number: 91-65165
ISBN: 0-89588-809-2

Manufactured in the United States of America

10 9 8 7 6 5 4 3 2 1

I dedicate this book to my parents.

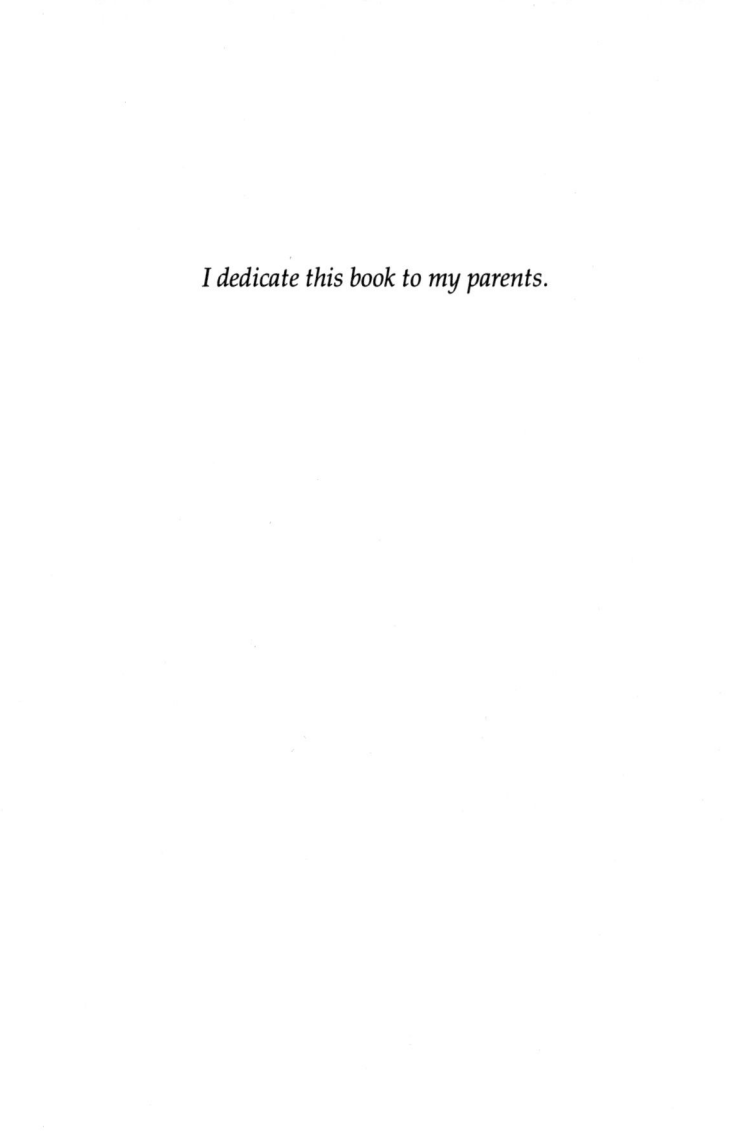

Acknowledgments

I wish to thank the following individuals, without whom this book would not have been possible:

Special thanks to Judith Bellamy, who did an excellent job of editing this book. Many thanks to Dianne King, Acquisitions Manager, who played an important role in getting this book published, and to Jim Compton, Series Editor, whose ideas substantially enhanced the manuscript. Also, thanks to Charles McHenry of Quarterdeck Office Systems, who provided copies of DESQview software.

Table of Contents

Introduction   xvii

Part I
AN INTRODUCTION TO DESQVIEW

Getting Around in DESQview	2
Starting DESQview	2
Displaying the DESQview Menu	2
Selecting Commands	3
Using the Windows in DESQview	4
Keyboard Usage	5
Concepts and Terminology	6
DESQview Compatibility	6
Mapping	7
Types of Memory	8
"Well-Behaved" and "Ill-Behaved" Programs	10
Running DESQview with Microsoft Windows 3	10

Part II
THE DESQVIEW MULTITASKING ENVIRONMENT

Add a Program	12
Auto Dialer	16
Big DOS	18
Change Colors	18
Change a Program	19

Close Window	20
Convert a Script	21
Delete a Program	22
DOS Services	23
DVANSI	27
Freeze	27
Help about DESQview	28
Hide	29
Learn: The Keystroke Macro Feature	30
Mark	34
Memory Status	35
Move	37
Open Window	38
Position	39
Put Aside	42
Quit DESQview	42
Rearrange	43
Resize	44
Scissors	45
Scroll	46
Setup DESQview	47
Specify Program Information	52
Switch Windows	59
Transfer	60
Tune Performance	61
Video Options	63
Zoom	64

Part III
QEMM, THE QUARTERDECK EXPANDED MEMORY MANAGER

Optimize	69
QEMM386.SYS	69
QEMM386.SYS ?	70
QEMM386.SYS ADAPTERRAM	70
QEMM386.SYS ADAPTERROM	71
QEMM386.SYS AUTO	72
QEMM386.SYS COMPAQ386S	72
QEMM386.SYS COMPAQEGAROM	73
QEMM386.SYS COMPAQHALFROM	74
QEMM386.SYS COMPAQROMMEMORY	74
QEMM386.SYS DISKBUF	75
QEMM386.SYS DMA	76
QEMM386.SYS DOS4	76
QEMM386.SYS EMBMEM	77
QEMM386.SYS EXCLUDE	77
QEMM386.SYS EXTMEM	78
QEMM386.SYS FORCEEMS	78
QEMM386.SYS FRAME	79
QEMM386.SYS FRAMELENGTH	80
QEMM386.SYS HANDLES	80
QEMM386.SYS HELP	81
QEMM386.SYS HMAMIN	81
QEMM386.SYS IGNOREA20	82
QEMM386.SYS INCLUDE	83
QEMM386.SYS LOCKDMA	83
QEMM386.SYS MAPS	84
QEMM386.SYS MEMORY	84
QEMM386.SYS NOCOMPAQFEATURES	85

QEMM386.SYS NOEMS	86
QEMM386.SYS NOFILL	86
QEMM386.SYS NOHMA	87
QEMM386.SYS NOPAUSEONERROR	87
QEMM386.SYS NOROM	88
QEMM386.SYS NOROMHOLES	88
QEMM386.SYS NOSHADOWRAM	89
QEMM386.SYS NOSORT	90
QEMM386.SYS NOTOPMEMORY	91
QEMM386.SYS NOVIDEOFILL	91
QEMM386.SYS NOVIDEORAM	92
QEMM386.SYS NOWINDOWS3	92
QEMM386.SYS NOXBDA	93
QEMM386.SYS NOXMS	93
QEMM386.SYS OFF	94
QEMM386.SYS OLDDV	95
QEMM386.SYS ON	95
QEMM386.SYS PAUSE	96
QEMM386.SYS RAM	96
QEMM386.SYS ROM	97
QEMM386.SYS TASKS	98
QEMM386.SYS UNUSUAL8042	98
QEMM386.SYS UNUSUALEXT	99
QEMM386.SYS VIDRAMEGA	100
QEMM386.SYS VIDRAMEMS	100
QEMM386.SYS WATCHDOG	101
QEMM.COM	102
QEMM.COM ?	102
QEMM.COM ACCESSED	103
QEMM.COM ACCESSED MAP	104
QEMM.COM ANALYSIS	105
QEMM.COM ANALYSIS MAP	106

QEMM.COM AUTO	106
QEMM.COM HELP	107
QEMM.COM MAP	107
QEMM.COM MEMORY	107
QEMM.COM NOPAUSEONERROR	108
QEMM.COM OFF	109
QEMM.COM ON	109
QEMM.COM PAUSE	109
QEMM.COM RESET	110
QEMM.COM SUMMARY	110
QEMM.COM TYPE	110
QEMM.COM TYPE MAP	111
LOADHI	112
LOADHI ?	113
LOADHI BESTFIT	113
LOADHI EXCLUDELARGEST	114
LOADHI EXCLUDEREGION	114
LOADHI EXCLUDESMALLEST	114
LOADHI GETSIZE	115
LOADHI HAPPIEST	115
LOADHI HELP	116
LOADHI LARGEST	116
LOADHI LO	116
LOADHI NOLO	117
LOADHI NOPAUSEONERROR	117
LOADHI PAUSE	117
LOADHI REGION	118
LOADHI SIZE	118
LOADHI SMALLEST	119
LOADHI TERMINATERESIDENT	119
The DOS Resource Programs	119
BUFFERS.COM	120

FCBS.COM	121
FILES.COM	122
LASTDRIVE.COM	122
The VIDRAM Program	123
VIDRAM ?	124
VIDRAM HELP	124
VIDRAM NOCGA	125
VIDRAM NOEGA	125
VIDRAM NOPAUSEONERROR	126
VIDRAM OFF	126
VIDRAM ON	126
VIDRAM PAUSE	127
VIDRAM RESIDENT	127
VIDRAM VIDRAMEGA	128
VIDRAM VIDRAMEMS	128
EMS2EXT.SYS	128

Part IV
MANIFEST MEMORY ANALYZER

DESQview Memory Status	133
DESQview Overview	134
DOS Drivers	135
DOS Environment	135
DOS Files	137
DOS Overview	137
Exit Exit	138
Exit Stay Resident	139
Expanded Benchmark	140
Expanded Handles	140
Expanded Overview	141

Expanded Pages	142
Expanded Timings	143
Extended Overview	144
Extended XMS	145
First Meg BIOS Data	146
First Meg Interrupts	146
First Meg Overview	148
First Meg Programs	149
First Meg Timings	150
Help	150
Hints Detail	151
Hints Overview	152
QEMM-386 ACCESSED	152
QEMM-386 ANALYSIS	153
QEMM-386 MEMORY	154
QEMM-386 OVERVIEW	154
QEMM-386 TYPE	155
System Adapters	156
System AUTOEXEC	156
System CMOS	157
System CONFIG	157
System Overview	158
Index	159

Introduction

The idea behind this book is simple. When you are stymied by a command in DESQview that doesn't work as you expected, or when you want a quick refresher about a certain procedure, you need a single source of information that can quickly help you solve the problem at hand and let you get on with your work.

DESQview Instant Reference is intended to give you briefly the essential information necessary to get the most from DESQview's numerous features—both the basic commands and the sophisticated functions that you may not use on a daily basis. It covers version 2.3 of both standard DESQview and DESQview 386, the enhancement designed to take advantage of the powerful 80386, 80386SX, and 80486 microprocessors. Since DESQview 386 comes packaged with two additional programs, QEMM-386 and Manifest, the book covers them as well.

DESQview, the main program, is probably the one you are most familiar with. QEMM-386, available separately or packaged with DESQview 386, is a memory manager. It works silently in the background, controlling your computer's memory and helping DESQview work efficiently. Manifest, also available either separately or as part of the DESQview 386 package, is an analysis tool. It gives you valuable information about your computer system and how to optimize it.

This book is not intended to replace the documentation included with DESQview or its related programs. It is neither an introduction to the programs nor a tutorial, but a reference for solving day-to-day application problems. It assumes you have installed DESQview and use it regularly. If you'd like comprehensive information about DESQview, read the manual or look for *Mastering DESQview* by Rick Altman, SYBEX, 1991.

USING THIS BOOK

This DESQview Instant Reference is divided into four parts. The first one introduces DESQview, as well as some of the basic terms and concepts you'll need to know to use the book. The three parts that follow cover DESQview, QEMM-386, and Manifest. Each part provides descriptions of all the commands or parameters, organized alphabetically, that are used for that program.

Each command or parameter entry starts with a short description of its purpose, followed by a sequence of steps or the keystrokes required to accomplish the purpose. Many entries also include a section headed Notes, containing additional information that will help you use the command or parameter, and a section of cross-references to other parts of the book that discuss related subjects. Some entries include a descriptive list of options to use with the command or parameter, or a short section of examples.

CONVENTIONS USED IN THIS BOOK

Keystrokes that you enter at your computer keyboard while you're working with a menu are printed in **boldface** type. (Part I, *An Introduction to DESQview,* describes the methods for selecting commands from menus.)

Keystrokes that you enter on a command line (such as at the DOS prompt or in a system or a batch file) are printed in a

different type style

and appear on a line by themselves.

Definitions or explanations of terms are printed in *italics*.

The key that completes most menu entries, and that may be labeled either Return or Enter on your keyboard, is represented by the symbol ⏎.

Part I

An Introduction to DESQview

Parts II, III, and IV of this book present the commands of the three programs that make up the DESQview package from Quarterdeck Office Systems: DESQview, QEMM-386, and Manifest. DESQview is the "main program," the operating environment you'll use to run and switch between application programs. QEMM, the Quarterdeck Expanded Memory Manager, takes control of your computer's memory resources, including expanded and extended memory. Experienced users can take advantage of its optional parameters to "fine-tune" this memory management; novices will do best to let QEMM run automatically. Manifest is a program that displays various statistics about your system's use of memory, hardware, and software. Anyone can run it, but interpreting the information it provides may require a more extensive background than a book of this scope can provide.

This part of the book is addressed primarily to less-experienced DESQview users. It briefly summarizes the mechanics of working with the menu system and defines some of the essential DESQview terminology used throughout the book.

2 An Introduction to DESQview

GETTING AROUND IN DESQVIEW

The main DESQview program allows you to "multitask," or run multiple programs in multiple windows at the same time. Once you have opened several windows, you can easily switch from one program to another, using only a few keystrokes.

With DESQview 386, you have the added capability of being able to run graphics and character-based programs side by side. DESQview 386 also taps into the special features of the 80386 microprocessor, such as allowing "well-behaved," "ill-behaved," and graphics programs to run simultaneously without interfering with each other. This means that you won't have to stop executing one program when you want to work in another.

STARTING DESQVIEW

Start DESQview by typing **DV** and pressing ↵ from the root directory of your hard drive. DOS loads the DV.COM program, which in turn loads the DV.EXE program in "high memory." (See *Types of Memory* later in this section for a description of high memory.) In earlier versions of DESQview, you typed XDV to achieve the same result, but in version 2.3, DV and XDV are identical.

The screen clears and the DESQview menu appears, as shown in Figure I.1. The bar cursor, a reverse video highlight bar, is located over the default menu choice. If you have a mouse installed, a diamond-shaped mouse cursor appears to the left of the menu selection, within the bar cursor. You will notice one-letter keystroke abbreviations listed to the right of each menu selection. A missing letter indicates that the command is not currently available.

DISPLAYING THE DESQVIEW MENU

To execute any of the DESQview commands presented in Part II of this book, you begin at a common starting point, the DESQview

Getting Around in DESQview 3

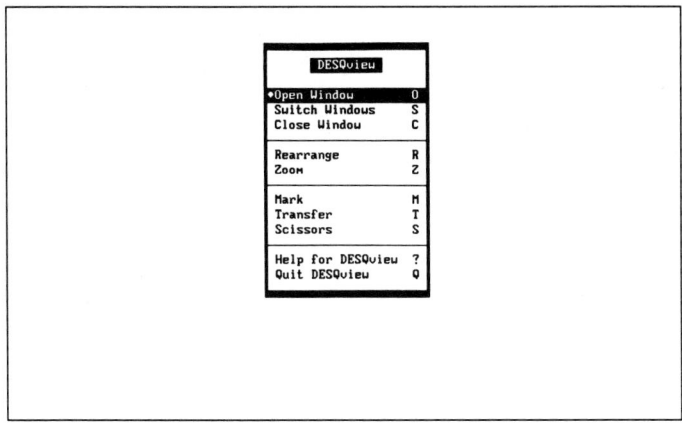

Figure I.1: The DESQview menu

menu. If it's not already on your screen, use one of the following commands to display this menu:

- Press the **Alt** key. (Quarterdeck calls this the DESQ key to remind you of its special use in DESQview. If you need to reserve the Alt key for some other purpose, you can assign the DESQ role to another key, as described under the "Change system keys?" option of the *Setup DESQview* entry in Part II. However, the Alt key usually works best.)

- If you have a two-button mouse, click both buttons simultaneously. On a three-button mouse, click the middle button.

SELECTING COMMANDS

There are several ways to select a command from any menu in DESQview.

- Type the character or characters listed to the right of the command you want to select; this is the fastest method.

- Use the arrow keys to move the bar cursor over the option you want and press either ↵ or the spacebar.

4 An Introduction to DESQview

- Move your mouse until the bar cursor is on the command you want and click the left mouse button to select it.

You can use the mouse and keyboard interchangeably to make menu selections.

USING THE WINDOWS IN DESQVIEW

If the current program's active window is not running full-screen, it is displayed with a double-line border to distinguish it from other windows you may have open. Other open windows are called background windows. Much of Part II is devoted to the tasks you can perform with and upon windows in DESQview. Here's a brief summary of the most important operations:

Opening: To run any program you've installed, you open its window. See *Open Window.*

Closing: To exit a program you're running, close its window. Note that a few programs (such as WordPerfect and Lotus 1-2-3, release 3.1) require you to use their own exit procedures instead. See *Close Window.*

Freezing: To halt the program running in the active window, freeze it. See *Freeze.*

Hiding: To remove a window from the screen temporarily without closing it, you hide it. See *Hide.*

Moving: To change the position of the window on the screen, you move it. See *Move.*

Resizing: To change the size of the window on the screen, you resize it. See *Resize.*

Scrolling: To see a different part of the program's screen display, you scroll the program in its window. See *Scroll.*

Switching: To change from one active window to another, you switch windows. See *Switch Windows.*

Transferring Information between Programs: To cut and paste information between two or more different programs that are not aware of each other, you transfer information.

Getting Around in DESQview 5

KEYBOARD USAGE

DESQview uses certain keys in the following ways:

DESQ displays the DESQview menu. The DESQ key is usually defined to be the Alt key. See *Displaying the DESQview Menu* above.

Learn is used to start and finish keyboard scripts. The Learn key is usually defined to be the key combination Shift-DESQ (unless you've redefined the DESQ key as something other than Alt. See *Learn* in Part II.).

↵ selects the current entry on a DESQview menu.

Spacebar selects the current entry on a DESQview menu.

Esc cancels a menu selection.

↑ moves the menu cursor to the previous entry above the cursor position.

↓ moves the menu cursor to the next entry below the current cursor position.

Ctrl allows you to simulate a mouse if you don't have one. The diamond-shaped mouse cursor will appear, and you can then control the cursor with the arrow keys.

Ctrl-NumLock suspends or freezes the program running in the current window.

Pause suspends or freezes your entire system.

Print-Screen causes the current image on the screen to be sent to your printer.

Ctrl-Alt-Del aborts execution of the active window and closes it.

Ctrl-Shift-Del aborts whatever you are doing in DESQview and restarts your system.

When you're at a DESQview menu with fill-in fields, use the following keys:

↵ completes a menu entry.

Tab moves the cursor to the next menu entry.

Shift-Tab moves the cursor to the previous menu entry.

Ctrl-End erases the field blank from the current position of the cursor to the end of the blank.

Home moves the cursor to the first field in the window.

End moves the cursor to the space following the last character in the field.

Arrow keys move the cursor up, down, left, or right within the menu area.

Esc cancels the currently displayed menu.

Backspace erases backward from the cursor, one character at a time.

Delete erases forward from the cursor, one character at a time.

Insert toggles the keyboard between insert mode and overwrite mode.

When you're working with the DESQview Learn feature, use the following keys:

` (the accent key) tells DESQview that the next key you press should not be used to record a script. It is called the Quoting character.

Ctrl-Break aborts the current script.

CONCEPTS AND TERMINOLOGY

The following paragraphs briefly explain some of the most important concepts, employed throughout this book and DESQview's documentation, that may be unfamiliar to novice users.

DESQVIEW COMPATIBILITY

A program written expressly for use with DESQview is called a DESQview-specific program. Such a program uses all the advanced features of DESQview and will run only in DESQview. Examples of

Concepts and Terminology 7

some DESQview-specific programs are those which come in a package called the DESQview Companions; they include DESQview Calc, DESQview Datebook, DESQview Link, and DESQview Notepad.

Most DOS programs can be used with DESQview without any problem, especially if you are using DESQview 386. They can run full-screen, or they can usually be resized into a window. Some programs, however, cannot operate properly in a window because they will not allow you to change a window's size using the commands available with DESQview. These are considered "ill-behaved" or "not DESQview-aware" programs. See *"Well-behaved" and "Ill-behaved" Programs* below for more information.

MAPPING

The terms "mapping," "remap," "mappable," "mapped," and "map" are used in different ways throughout this book. *Mapping* means to identify a section of memory by its address, or location, and to change, or *remap*, the address. This allows unused areas of memory to be redirected to locations where they will be more easily accessible, either for storing data or for DOS to use in running programs. QEMM-386, DESQview's memory manager, is the utility that performs these mapping functions. (See *Types of Memory* in Part I and Part III, *QEMM, The Quarterdeck Expanded Memory Manager*.)

Mappable areas of memory are unused addresses, usually in high memory, which can be made available to DOS by the expanded or extended memory specifications. (See the following section on *Types of Memory*.)

The term *mapped key* refers to a single key that represents a series of keystrokes, called a script, created by DESQview's Learn feature. (See *Learn: The Keystroke Macro Feature* in Part II.)

Under QEMM-386 and Manifest, DESQview's memory analysis program, a *map* is a graphic display of information about the use of memory in your computer. (See Part III and Part IV, *Manifest Memory Analyzer*.)

TYPES OF MEMORY

Memory is arranged in three basic classes on PC-compatible computers: conventional memory, expanded memory, and extended memory. While all memory is physically the same, the way your computer uses and accesses each type is radically different.

Conventional memory extends from 0K to 1024K, but only the first 640K has traditionally been available to DOS for running programs. The most commonly used and the most accessible type of memory, conventional memory is used by terminate-and-stay-resident programs (TSRs) as well as by DOS. TSRs stay in memory after they are executed and closed, rather than terminating and freeing the memory they occupied. Thus they remain quickly accessible at the press of a key combination while you're working in other programs; they also support device drivers, such as the one that allows you to use a mouse.

The area from 640K to 1024K, called *"high memory"* or *"high RAM,"* is occupied by system ROM, video memory, hardware drivers, and the EMS page frame.

Expanded memory, often referred to as EMS, is memory accessed by software called an Expanded Memory Specification driver. This was a method developed to give early machines access to greater memory than their normal 640K limit. It is still used, but it makes available expanded memory only in small blocks, or "pages." EMS maps a 64K section of high memory and, in effect, borrows it for the storage of data from an application program.

Extended memory is available only with computers based on the 286 or later microprocessors, which have been designed to access much more memory than their earlier relatives. It is located above conventional memory. To access this additional memory, the XMS extended memory specification was designed. It defines three areas of memory: HMA (the high memory area—not to be confused with "high memory" discussed above), UMB (upper memory blocks), and EMB (extended memory blocks).

Concepts and Terminology 9

DOS 5 enables you to take advantage of three areas of memory that were previously unavailable:

HMA is a 64K block of memory starting at the very beginning of extended memory (1024K). It is used to enable application programs, which are normally restricted to the conventional memory area below 1024K, to be loaded and executed in extended memory. The result is an additional 64K of addressable DOS memory space.

UMB is extended memory mapped into unused areas of high memory (above 640K and below 1024K) for running programs. It is more accessible to programs than is the extended memory area above 1024K.

EMB refers to any remaining extended memory available (after HMA and UMB have taken their share) for allocation as extended memory.

Figure I.2 shows a pictorial representation of memory. Notice that extended memory fills up to 16 megabytes on a 286 machine and up to 4 gigabytes (4000 megabytes) on a 386 machine. Expanded memory does not appear in the picture because it is an addressing specification, rather than a fixed location in memory.

Most programs are limited to 640K for program codes. Most can use only expanded or only extended memory for storing data, but

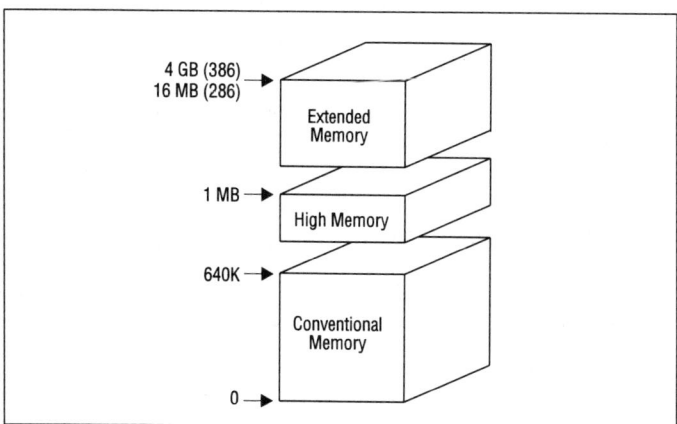

Figure I.2: The three types of memory

some programs can use both types. QEMM supports all memory drivers for each type of memory just discussed.

"WELL-BEHAVED" AND "ILL-BEHAVED" PROGRAMS

Two terms are used to refer to the ways video information is displayed by programs in DESQview.

Well-behaved describes a program that writes to a memory buffer rather than directly to the screen. DESQview then accesses this memory buffer to display information in the program's window.

Ill-behaved refers to a program that writes directly to the screen. DESQview has a hard time running ill-behaved programs in a window because they try to write on the screen outside their window. The DESQview package contains files that include special drivers that allow some ill-behaved programs to work correctly in DESQview.

RUNNING DESQVIEW WITH MICROSOFT WINDOWS 3

An important advantage of DESQview version 2.3 over earlier versions is its ability to run Microsoft Windows 3.0 in two of its three modes, "real" and "standard." (Since the third mode, "enhanced," duplicates DESQview's support for standard DOS applications within a windows environment, you can't use it with DESQview.) To use MS Windows in its real or standard mode, you add the appropriate program to DESQview's Open Window menu. The DESQview package contains files with the basic information needed to install and run both MS Windows 3 Real and MS Windows 3 Standard. See the *Add a Program* and *Open Window* entries in Part II for the appropriate procedures.

Part II
The DESQview Multitasking Environment

DESQview's multitasking environment allows you to run multiple programs in multiple windows on your screen at one time. Once you have opened several windows, you can easily switch from one program to another, using only a few keystrokes. The DESQview commands discussed in this section are organized alphabetically for easy reference.

ADD A PROGRAM

• **PURPOSE**   Lets you add a program to the list contained on the Open Window menu, illustrated in Figure II.1 (note that the programs listed in the illustration may differ from those listed on your Open Window menu). This procedure must be followed once for every program you would like to run in DESQview.

```
           Open Window
  ◆AutoCAD                    AC
   BASIC                      BA
   Big DOS                    BD
   Convert a Script           CS
   DESQview Calc              DC
   DOS (128K)                 D1
   DOS Services               DS
   GrandView                  GU
   Instant Recall             IR
   Lotus Agenda               LA
   Memory Status              MS
   MS Windows 3 Real Mode     WR
   MS Windows 3 Std. Mode     W3
   Paradox 3                  PD
   PC Shell                   SH
   PC Tools Desktop           DT
   More                       PgDn

   Add a Program              AP
   Delete a Program           DP
   Change a Program           CP
```

Figure II.1: The Open Window menu

DESQview needs certain basic information about any program it is to run. Adding a program to the Open Window menu makes this information available to DESQview. The DESQview package includes files containing this basic information for over 120 DOS and DESQview-specific programs (a listing of these follows). DESQview will automatically install Big DOS, DOS Services, Memory Status, Manifest, and any program on the list that is already on your hard drive. To add one of the other listed programs, you simply select it from the Add a Program list. To add a program that's not on the list, you must supply the information yourself by filling in the Specify Program Information screen, using a copy of the program's documentation.

Programs for Which DESQview Has Basic Information

Alarm Clock	Fast Graphs
askSam	Folio Views
AutoCAD	FoxBASE Plus
AutoCAD 386	FoxPro
BASIC	Framework II
BASICA	Framework III
Big DOS	Freelance Plus 2
BRIEF Editor	Freelance Plus 3
Byline	GEM Desktop
Clarion	GrandView
Connection CoProc	HAL & 1-2-3 Release 2
Convert a Script	Harvard Graphics
CrossTalk	Higgins
DataEase	IBM Interleaf
dBASE II	Lotus 1-2-3 1A
dBASE III Plus	Lotus 1-2-3 Release 2
dBASE IV	Lotus 1-2-3 Release 3
DeskMate	Lotus Agenda
DESQview Calc	Lotus Express
DESQview Datebook	Lotus Graph 1A
DESQview Link	Lotus Metro
DESQview Notepad	Lotus Signal 2.1
DESQView Palette	Magellan
DisplayWrite 4	Manuscript
DOS (128K)	Memory Status
DOS 4 Shell	MHS Mail Server
DOS Services	MS Excel
Enable	MS Windows 2

14 The DESQview Multitasking Environment

Programs for Which DESQview Has Basic Information

MS Windows 3	PFS:Report
MS Windows 3	PFS:Write
MS Word 4.0	ProComm Plus
MS Word 5.0	Q&A
MultiMate	Q&A Write
MultiMate Advantage	Qmodem
Multiplan	Quarterdeck Manifest
Norton Commander	Quattro
Norton Utilities 3	Quicken 2
Norton Utilities 4	Quicken 3
OfficeWriter	R:BASE
PageMaker	R:BASE for DOS
Paradox 1.0	R:BASE System V
Paradox 1.1	Rapid File
Paradox 2	Ready!
Paradox 3	Real Mode
Paradox 386	Reflex
PC Outline	Reflex Report
PC Paint	Sample Document
PC Talk III	Sample Sprdsheet
PC Tools Desktop	Setup DESQview
PC Tools Shell	SideKick
PFS:ACCESS Version B	SideKick Plus
PFS:File	Sideways
PFS:Graph	Sprint 1.00
PFS:Plan	Sprint 1.01
PFS:Professional Plan	Standard Mode
PFS:Professional Write	Storyboard Plus

Add a Program

Programs for Which DESQview Has Basic Information

SuperCalc 4
SuperCalc 5
Symphony
The Coordinator
The Coordinator 2
ThinkTank
Ventura Professional 2.0
Ventura Publisher
Widespread
WordPerfect 4.2
WordPerfect 5
WordStar 2000 Release 3
WordStar 3.3
WordStar 4.0
WordStar Professional 5
WordStar/CorrectStar
XyWrite III Plus

Once you add a program, it will appear on the Open Window menu of DESQview. You can then open the program at any time and execute it.

To Add a Program to the Open Window Menu

1. Display the DESQview menu, as described in Part I, and select **O**pen Window.

2. Select **A**dd a **P**rogram from the Open Window menu.

3. Use the **PgUp** and **PgDn** keys to scroll between pages of the programs available.

4. Select the program you want to install, using either the keyboard or the mouse, and press the **spacebar** while the cursor is located over the program name.

5. Continue to mark program names as described in Step 4 if you want to add more than one program at a time.

6. Press ↵ after you have selected all the programs you want to add to the Open Window menu. You will be prompted to enter a path name for each program you just marked.

7. Type the standard DOS path telling DESQview where the program is located on your hard drive.

16   The DESQview Multitasking Environment

8. Press ↵ or click the left mouse button over DONE on the menu to return to the application you were using in DESQview before you started the Add a Program procedure or to the DESQview menu if you were not in an application.

To Add a Program That Is Not Listed

1. Display the DESQview menu, as described in Part I, and select **O**pen Window.

2. Select **A**dd a **P**rogram from the Open Window menu.

3. Select **O**ther from the Add a Program menu.

4. Type the name of the subdirectory where the program may be found on your computer's hard drive, and press ↵. If DESQview finds a .PIF or a .DVP file in the subdirectory, it will display that program's name as an option.

5. Fill out the information in the Specify Program Information screen, and press ↵. See *Specify Program Information* for the full procedure.

See Also   *Change a Program, Convert a Script, Delete a Program, Memory Status, Open Window, Specify Program Information*

AUTO DIALER

- **PURPOSE**   Marks a telephone number from the active window and dials it.

To Dial a Telephone Number

1. Begin in a program (such as a database) that contains the telephone number you want to dial. Make sure the number appears in the active window.

Auto Dialer 17

2. Display the DESQview menu, as described in Part I, and select **M**ark.

3. Move the DESQview cursor with the keyboard or mouse to the first digit of the telephone number you want to dial.

4. Type **P** to select Mark Phone #, and DESQview will highlight the whole telephone number string.

5. Select **D**ial from the Mark menu.

6. Press ↵ for a local call, or select one of up to three long-distance access codes you've predefined. (See Notes below for more information about access codes.)

7. As soon as DESQview has dialed the number, pick up the phone, and select the **T**alk menu option.

- **NOTES** In order to use the Auto Dialer, you must have a modem, preferably Hayes-compatible, and it must be set up correctly. This includes telling DESQview which communications port your modem is connected to. (See *Setup DESQview.*) Most modems have a built-in speaker, so you can hear the computer as it dials. If your modem does not have a speaker, it will be difficult to use this procedure.

The telephone number string consists of three or more digits and ends when DESQview finds two spaces or a letter. Examples of valid telephone number strings include 123-4567, (800)227-2346, and 916 898-4636.

Before dialing a telephone number, DESQview can precede it with an access code, consisting of whatever sequence of digits you dial to access your long-distance telephone carrier (such as AT&T, MCI, or Sprint). If your modem is connected through an office phone system, the access code may include the "9" (or other number) required to reach an outside line. You define access codes in setting up your modem with DESQview.

See Also *Setup DESQview*

BIG DOS

- **PURPOSE**   Lets you work in DESQview at the DOS command line. When you start Big DOS, you can do anything you would be able to do if you were at the DOS prompt and were not running DESQview. Big DOS gives you approximately 640K of memory (minus some DOS memory overhead) to run your programs.

To Open a Big DOS Window

1. Display the DESQview menu, as described in Part I, and select **O**pen Window.

2. Select **B**ig **D**os from the list of programs. A DOS window will be opened.

3. Use any DOS command and run any DOS application.

See Also   *Close Window, DVANSI, Open Window*

CHANGE COLORS

- **PURPOSE**   Temporarily changes the colors of DESQview's active window or menu if you have a color monitor.

To Change the Colors of a DESQview Window

1. Display the DESQview menu, as described in Part I, and select **R**earrange.

2. Select **C**hange Colors from the Rearrange menu.

3. Use the left and right arrow keys to change the color of the text, and use the up and down arrow keys to change the background color.

Change a Program   19

4. Press ↵ when you are satisfied with the appearance of the window.

To Change the Colors of the DESQview Menus

1. Close all open windows.
2. Display the DESQview menu, as described in Part I, and select **Rearrange**.
3. Select **Change Colors** from the Rearrange menu.
4. Use the left and right arrow keys to change the color of the text in the menu; use the up and down arrow keys to change the background color of the menu.
5. Press ↵ when you are satisfied with the appearance of the menu.

• **NOTES**   The changes you make using this method are only temporary and don't affect programs that run in a full screen. To change the DESQview colors permanently or to change full-screen colors, run the Setup DESQview program.

See Also   *Close Window, Rearrange, Setup DESQview*

CHANGE A PROGRAM

• **PURPOSE**   Gives you access to an application program's Specify Program Information screens. Use it to modify any of the information DESQview has about a program.

To Modify Information about a Program

1. Display the DESQview menu, as described in Part I, and select **Open Window**.

The DESQview Multitasking Environment

2. Select Change a Program from the Open Window menu.
3. Select the program whose information you want to modify. The Specify Program Information standard options menu (illustrated in the *Specify Program Information* entry) will be displayed, showing the current information about the program you've selected.
4. Modify the options you want changed.
5. Press **F1** if you need to display the Specify Program Information Advanced Options menu (also shown in the *Specify Program Information* entry), and make any changes necessary.
6. Press the ↵ key when finished. If any field is filled out incorrectly, DESQview will alert you and let you change the entry. The new information will be written to the program information file.

- **NOTES** Programs installed directly from the Add a Program menu usually do not need to be modified, but those you install yourself sometimes need adjustment before they work correctly.

See Also *Add a Program, Delete a Program, Specify Program Information, Tune Performance*

CLOSE WINDOW

- **PURPOSE** Shuts down the program in the active window. Before closing a window, you should save any files that you want to keep.

To Close the Active Window

1. Make sure that you have finished whatever you were doing and have saved any open files.

2. Display the DESQview menu, as described in Part I, and select Close Window.

3. Confirm that you really want to close the window by answering Yes to the prompt.

• **NOTES** The confirmation prompt that DESQview displays after you choose Close Window is a safeguard to prevent your accidentally closing a window and losing any valuable data.

Some programs, such as WordPerfect and Lotus 1-2-3, release 3.1, do not accept DESQview's Close Window command. To close the window from these programs, simply exit the program as you normally would, and DESQview will automatically close the window.

See Also *Big DOS, Change Colors, Open Window, Quit DESQview, Switch Windows*

CONVERT A SCRIPT

• **PURPOSE** Allows you to convert a Learn script from its special DESQview-encoded format to a regular ASCII text file and vice versa. Use this DESQview utility program to look at and modify Learn scripts.

To Convert a Script

1. Display the DESQview menu, as described in Part I, and select Open Window.

2. Select Convert a Script from the list of programs.

3. Select **S** to convert a script to a text file or **T** to convert a text file to a script.

22 The DESQview Multitasking Environment

4. Enter the name of the file you want to convert *from*, and press ↵.

5. Enter the name of the file you want to convert *to*, and press ↵. Make sure you don't enter the same file name twice, or the file might be overwritten and lost.

6. The file will be converted and written to the new file.

7. Select **X** to terminate the Convert a Script program.

• **NOTES** Many times it is useful to be able to see the scripts you have created and to edit them. Other times you can create scripts in a text editor and then convert them to a script file.

To use the Convert a Script program, you must first add it to the Open Window menu. See *Add a Program* for more information.

See Also *Add a Program, Learn*

DELETE A PROGRAM

• **PURPOSE** Displays a list of all the programs you can run in DESQview and allows you to delete a program from the list if you no longer want to use it in DESQview.

To Remove a Program from the Open Window Menu

1. Display the DESQview menu, as described in Part I, and select **Open Window**.

2. Select **Delete a Program** from the Open Window menu.

3. Select the program you want to remove from the menu. A message appears asking you to confirm that you want to delete the selected program.

4. Press ↵ to confirm deletion, or press **Esc** to abort the process.

5. If you press ↵, the program will be removed from the DESQview Open Window menu.

• **NOTES** Deleting a program from the Open Window menu does not delete it from your disk; you can still run the program from DOS in its usual manner. To remove the program from your drive, use the DOS command **Del** or the DESQview DOS Services equivalent function.

See Also *Add a Program, Change a Program, DOS Services, Open Window*

DOS SERVICES

• **PURPOSE** Gives you access to many features of DOS while in DESQview. A DESQview-specific utility program, it helps you manage the files on your system, using menus to select DOS functions instead of typing commands at the DOS prompt.

To Start the DOS Services Program

1. Display the DESQview menu, as described in Part I, and select **O**pen Window.

2. Select **DOS S**ervices from the list of programs. The DOS Services window appears on the left side of your screen, and the DOS Services menu appears in the upper-right corner, as illustrated in Figure II.2.

3. You can now use the functions found on the DOS Services menu. They are described in the Options section below.

24 The DESQview Multitasking Environment

```
┌1═DOS═Services══════════════════════┐  ┌──────────────────────┐
│    PgUp  PgDn   ↑    ↓   ^Home  ^End│  │     DOS Services     │
│Directory of C:\dv (Hard Drive)     │  │                      │
│1190583 bytes in 85 files, 18178048 fre│ │ Directory         D  │
│                                    │  │                      │
│ •.            <DIR>    1-06-91  6:12p│ │ Append            A  │
│ ..            <DIR>    1-06-91  6:12p│ │ Backup            B  │
│ CALC          <DIR>    1-06-91  6:13p│ │ Copy              C  │
│ AU-PIF  BAK    416     1-27-91  2:06p│ │ Erase             E  │
│ SETUP   BAT     43     1-13-91  6:52p│ │ Print             P  │
│ AU-LOAD COM    960     9-07-90  2:31a│ │ Rename            R  │
│ AUTOINST COM  3029     9-07-90  2:31a│ │ Type              T  │
│ CONUSCR COM   6068     9-07-90  2:31a│ │                      │
│ DEVICE  COM    638     9-07-90  2:31a│ │ Mark by Name      M  │
│ DOSSERV COM  17296     9-07-90  2:31a│ │ Only Show Marked  O  │
│ DV      COM   9751     9-07-90  2:31a│ │ Unmark by Name    U  │
│ DVANSI  COM   2016     9-07-90  2:31a│ │                      │
│ DVHERC  COM   1784     9-07-90  2:31a│ │ More              »  │
│ DVPAL   COM   4079     9-07-90  2:31a│ │                      │
│ DVREG   COM    394     9-07-90  2:31a│ └──────────────────────┘
│ DVSETUP COM  14332     9-07-90  2:31a│
│ FV-LOAD COM    693     9-07-90  2:31a│
│ INSTLAC COM  17088     9-07-90  2:31a│
│ LS-LOAD COM   2833     9-07-90  2:31a│
└────────────────────────────────────┘
```

Figure II.2: The DOS Services screen

To Display a Sorted Directory in DOS Services

1. Start the DOS Services program, as instructed in the previous procedure.

2. Select **D**irectory from the DOS Services menu.

3. Enter a regular DOS path name at the "Path" prompt on the Directory menu.

4. If you want to sort the directory, select **P**rimary Sort Key. A menu appears, listing the sorting options.

5. Select a primary sorting criterion from the Primary Sort Key menu. By selecting None or typing an **X**, you can choose not to sort. After you've selected an option, you are returned to the Directory menu.

6. If you want a secondary sorting criterion, select **S**econdary Sort Key.

7. Select the secondary sorting criterion you want to use in the same way you selected the primary sorting criterion.

DOS Services 25

8. Press ↵ from the Directory menu. The DOS Services window will list the files sorted in the manner you requested.

9. You may now use the other commands found on the DOS Services menu and submenus to perform specific operations on the files listed in the window.

To Mark Files for Manipulation Using DOS Services Menu Commands

1. Display a directory in the manner described in the previous procedure.

2. To mark files using the keyboard, move the bar cursor with the arrow keys over the file you want to mark, and press ↵ or the **spacebar**. If you marked the wrong file, you may unmark it by moving the bar cursor over the file a second time and pressing ↵ or the **spacebar** again.

3. To mark files using the mouse, move the diamond-shaped mouse cursor over the file you want to mark, and click the left mouse button.

To Exit DOS Services

- Select **C**lose Window from the DESQview menu.

Options

Directory displays a list of files for a given directory in the program window.

Append joins two or more files together.

Backup lets you back up files from your hard disk to floppy disks.

Copy makes a copy of one or more files.

Erase deletes files from the currently displayed directory.

Print uses the DOS PRINT program to send files to your printer in the background, so you don't have to wait while your printer is operating.

Rename allows you to change the name of any file.

Type displays the contents of a file.

More displays a second menu, listing the following additional, less frequently used options. Use the mouse or press the asterisk (*) key to select More.

Change Directory lets you change the default drive or directory used by the other commands.

Make Directory creates a new subdirectory on the current drive.

Remove Directory erases an existing directory.

Copy Diskette makes a complete copy of a floppy diskette.

Format Diskette initializes a new diskette before you use it on your computer.

Restore Backup restores files saved using the Backup command.

• **NOTES** DOS Services differs from Big DOS in that you use menus to access DOS functions and you cannot execute programs from DOS Services.

All of the commands available through the DOS Services menus work in a manner similar to that of their DOS counterparts. The commands found on the menus operate on a single marked file or on several marked files at once. See the Options section for information about these commands.

If you want to use a DOS command that is not included on the menus, use the Other command found on the More DOS Services menu. To access More DOS Services, press the asterisk (*) twice from the main DOS Services menu. This will let you type any DOS command in a prompt.

See Also   *Delete a Program, Open Window*

DVANSI

- **PURPOSE** Replaces the ANSI.SYS device driver when you're working in a DOS window while using DESQview.

To Install DVANSI

1. Open a Big DOS window, as described in the *Big DOS* entry.
2. Type **DVANSI** from the DOS command line, and press ↵. The equivalent of the ANSI.SYS driver is installed.
3. You may now take full advantage of any programs that use the ANSI control codes to manipulate the screen.

- **NOTES** Big DOS in a DESQview window ignores any ANSI.SYS file that was loaded as a device driver in your CONFIG.SYS configuration file upon booting up. You must run the DVANSI program to achieve the same result when working in DESQview.

You can leave ANSI.SYS in your CONFIG.SYS file, as it may be convenient at times when you are not working in DESQview. If you find yourself loading DVANSI every time you open a DOS window in DESQview, you might consider creating a script to accomplish the loading automatically. See *Learn* for more information.

See Also *Big DOS, Learn*

FREEZE

- **PURPOSE** Halts the program running in the active window. The program will resume at the point where you froze it the next time you activate the window and press a key.

To Freeze a Window

1. Display the DESQview menu, as described in Part I, and select **Rearrange**.
2. Select Freeze from the Rearrange menu. The program in the active window will stop running.
3. Display the DESQview menu again, and switch to a different program.
4. Press any key except DESQ, Ctrl, or Shift-DESQ to resume the program when you switch back to the window you froze.

Shortcut Press the **Ctrl-NumLock** key combination from the active window to accomplish the freeze.

• **NOTES** Use this function to stop a program temporarily from running in the background. This is helpful when you are multitasking and you want the computer to dedicate all its processor time to a certain window but you don't want to close all open windows. Simply go to each window you aren't using and freeze it.

See Also *Rearrange*

HELP ABOUT DESQVIEW

• **PURPOSE** Provides online help any time you have a question about a DESQview function.

To Get Help

1. Display the DESQview menu, as described in Part I.
2. Select **?** to display the Help index.

3. Select a topic. Information about the topic will appear on the screen.

4. Press **?** to return to the DESQview menu when you are finished reading the Help screen.

5. Press **Esc** to return to the previous window you were working on.

● **NOTES** Within the Help screen, you may display the Help index by pressing the / key. Exit Help by pressing the **Esc** key.

HIDE

● **PURPOSE** Temporarily removes a window from the screen without closing it. The program in the window continues to run in the background.

To Hide a Window

1. Display the DESQview menu, as described in Part I, and select **R**earrange.

2. Select **H**ide from the Rearrange menu.

3. You will be switched to the application you were using in DESQview before you selected the Hide a Window option or to the DESQview Menu if you were not in an application. The program you just chose to hide continues to run in the background.

● **NOTES** To bring a hidden window back to the screen, use the Switch Windows option from the DESQview menu.

See Also *Put Aside, Rearrange, Switch Windows*

LEARN: THE KEYSTROKE MACRO FEATURE

- **PURPOSE** Records a keyboard script. A script is a sequence of keystrokes that DESQview memorizes and can execute whenever you press a particular key that you have redefined, known as the *mapped* key. You create scripts from the Learn menu. To display the Learn menu, hold down the **Shift** key and press the **DESQ** key (**Alt**, unless you've redefined it). This combination is called the **Learn key.**

DESQview allows you to create two types of scripts: a *program* script, which you create while running an application program in an open window; and a *global* script, which is created and which works only while a DESQview menu is displayed.

To Create a Program Script

1. Begin with your application in exactly the same state it will be in whenever you run the script. For example, an appropriate text, database, or spreadsheet file should be displayed, and the cursor should be placed where it will appear when the script begins executing.

2. Display the Learn menu by pressing the **Learn** key, described above.

3. Select Start Script. A message appears to remind you to press the key you want to redefine as the mapped key, with which you'll execute the script.

4. Press any key you choose.

5. Type a name for your script at the prompt that appears, and press ↵. The name is optional and is required only if you want to create a startup script. In this case, the first character must be an exclamation mark. If you don't name your script, DESQview will assign it a name based on the

Learn: The Keystroke Macro Feature 31

program's two-letter designation on the Open Window menu.

6. Everything you type from now on is recorded as part of your script.

7. Press the **Learn** key and select Finish Script from the Learn menu to end your script.

8. When you exit the program, DESQview will ask if you want to save the script to disk. Select **S**ave Scripts to use the script you created the next time you run your program in DESQview.

To Create a Global Script

1. Bring your cursor to the point in the DESQview menu system where you want the script to begin executing.

2. Display the Learn menu by pressing the **Learn** key, described in the Purpose section.

3. Select Start Script. A message appears asking you to press the key you want to redefine as the mapped key, with which you'll execute the script.

4. Press any key you choose.

5. Type a name for your script and press ↵. The name is optional, and is required only if you want to create a startup script. In this case, you must start the name with an exclamation mark. If you don't name your script, DESQview will assign it a name based on the program's two-letter designation on the Open Window menu.

6. Everything you type from now on is recorded as part of your script.

7. Press the **Learn** key and select Finish Script from the Learn menu to end the script.

8. When you exit DESQview, it will ask you if you want to save the script to disk. Select **S**ave Scripts to use the script you created the next time you run DESQview.

To Play Back a Program Script

1. Open the window of the program associated with the script.

2. Press the key the script is mapped to. The script will be played back on the screen.

To Play Back a Global Script

1. Display the DESQview menu, as described in Part I, or start from any DESQview menu that may be displayed.

2. Press the key the script is mapped to. The script will be played back on the screen.

To Abort Either a Global or a Program Script

- Press the **Ctrl-Break** key combination while the script is playing back to abort the script immediately.

To Display a List of Scripts

1. Display the Learn menu by pressing the **Learn** key, described in the Purpose section.

2. Select Display Scripts. A list of the scripts will appear. (You can play back a script by selecting it from the Script List.)

3. Press the **Esc** key to return to your program without playing back a script.

To Access Different Sets of Scripts in the Same Program

1. Display the Learn menu by pressing the **Learn** key, described in the Purpose section.

2. Select Load Scripts from the Learn menu.

Learn: The Keystroke Macro Feature

3. Enter the name of the script you want to access at the "Script Name" prompt.
4. Press ↵. The new script will be loaded.

To Delete a Script

1. Display the Learn menu by pressing the **Learn** key (described in the Purpose section) while you're in the program from which you want to delete a script.
2. Select Start Script from the Learn menu.
3. Press the mapped key for the script you want to delete.
4. Immediately select Finish Script to restore the mapped key to its original use.

• **NOTES** Edit. You edit a script by running DESQview's Convert a Script program. See *Convert a Script*.

"Learning" Signal. When DESQview is recording a script, each keystroke will make a click on your system speaker. This is to remind you that a script is being "learned."

Deactivate Playback. The ` key, also called the Quoting character, tells DESQview that the next key you press should not play back a script that's mapped to it. Normally, when you press a key you've redefined—for example, the F2 key—the key performs the script you mapped to that key. However, if you press the Quoting key immediately before pressing the F2 key, the original action of the F2 key is performed instead.

Buffers. While you are working on a script, it is temporarily stored in a special area of memory called the script buffer. (A buffer exists for every program running in your computer.) You are reminded to save your scripts when you exit the program if any changes have been made to the script buffer. To make sure you don't lose your scripts because of system failure, it is useful to tell DESQview to save the scripts buffer. When you start DESQview, the global scripts you created on DESQview menus and saved are automatically loaded. Likewise, when you open a program window, the saved scripts associated with that program are automatically loaded.

Pauses. To make scripts more useful, you can specify a pause during playback to allow some action to take place. To put a pause in your program, you select one of three options from the Learn menu as you are creating the script. A Fixed-Size Pause will temporarily stop playback to allow you to type a certain number of characters, and then the script will resume. A Variable Pause tells DESQview that, when the script is played back, you want to stop temporarily to type in a variable number of characters, and then resume the script when you select Variable Pause from the Learn menu. A Time Delay lets you halt playback of a script for a given number of seconds to view the display; typing additional characters at this point has no effect.

Startup Scripts. A particularly useful script in DESQview is called a startup script. A startup script works somewhat like the AUTOEXEC.BAT file on your hard drive does. It instructs DESQview to open several windows automatically at the time you start up either a program or DESQview.

You create a startup script just as you do any other DESQview script, except that when the Start a Script menu appears, you enter a name in the Script Name field that begins with an exclamation point. When recording a global startup script, be sure that no other windows are open.

See Also *Convert a Script, DVANSI, Setup DESQview, Transfer*

MARK

- **PURPOSE** Used in conjunction with the Transfer command to cut and paste information from the screen of a non-DESQview-specific program to the screen of any other program. The procedure is described in the *Transfer* entry of this book. To exchange information between DESQview-specific programs, use the Scissors command.

See Also *Scissors, Transfer*

MEMORY STATUS

- **PURPOSE** Displays the current memory usage of your system at any time.

To Run the Memory Status Program

1. Display the DESQview menu, as described in Part I, and select Open Window.

2. Select Memory Status from the list of programs. A window is opened showing a table that describes the utilization of memory in your computer.

To Exit the Memory Status Program

1. Make sure the Memory Status program occupies the active window by checking to see that its window has a double-line border.

2. Display the DESQview menu, as described in Part I, and select Close Window.

- **NOTES** The table that appears when you run the Memory Status program looks like Figure II.3 (except, of course, the numbers on your screen will probably be different). The row headings indicate three memory areas: common memory, conventional memory, and expanded memory. The columns list the current sizes of total memory, total memory available, and largest memory available in each memory area.

Common memory refers to the amount of memory used to store the information DESQview needs to manage windows and to do other housekeeping chores. *Conventional memory* is the memory available to run programs. *Expanded memory* refers to the memory provided by an additional memory board or made available by a memory manager, such as QEMM. It can also be used to run a program if

36 The DESQview Multitasking Environment

```
┌1═Memory═Status═══════════════════════════════════┐
│                                                  │
│                      Total    Total     Largest  │
│                      Memory   Available Available│
│                                                  │
│  Common Memory       17408    13864     13818    │
│                                                  │
│  Conventional Memory 583K     576K      566K     │
│                                                  │
│  Expanded Memory     2960K    2848K     560K     │
│                                                  │
└──────────────────────────────────────────────────┘
```

Figure II.3: The Memory Status display

you change the amount of memory allocated, using the Specify Program Information screen.

Total memory is the entire memory available in your system for a given memory category. *Total available* is the entire amount of memory available in a certain memory category at the current moment. The largest area of consecutive memory available to run a program at the current moment is labeled *Largest available*.

You will want to pay particular attention to two of the numbers displayed in the table. The number for "Largest Available Conventional Memory" gives the size of the largest program that can be loaded at the current time without swapping other programs out of memory. The number displayed under "Largest Available Expanded Memory" is the size of the largest program that can be run in expanded memory.

To use the Memory Status program, you must first add it to the Open Window menu. See *Add a Program* for more information.

See Also *Add a Program, Part IV: Manifest Memory Analyzer, Setup DESQview, Specify Program Information*

MOVE

- **PURPOSE** Changes the position of the active window on the screen. You may use either the keyboard or the mouse.

To Change the Position of the Active Window Using the Keyboard

1. Display the DESQview menu, as described in Part I, and select **Rearrange**.

2. Select Move from the Rearrange menu.

3. Use the arrow keys to reposition the active window on your screen.

4. Select DONE from the Move menu.

To Change the Position of the Active Window Using a Mouse

1. Move the mouse cursor to the top border of the active window, and click the left mouse button. The Move menu appears.

2. Move the window to its new location using the mouse.

3. Select DONE from the Move menu. The cursor will return to the active window in its new location.

- **NOTES** Of the two methods that can be used to change the position of the current window, usually it is easier to use the mouse. Sometimes a combination of the two methods works well, by having one hand on your mouse and the other hand on your keyboard.

See Also *Position, Rearrange, Resize, Scroll, Zoom*

# OPEN WINDOW

- **PURPOSE** Starts a program that has been installed in DESQview.

To Open a DESQview Window

1. Display the DESQview menu, as described in Part I.
2. Select Open Window.
3. Select the program you want to load from the list in the Open Window menu. The program will be executed immediately.

- **NOTES** The Open Window menu includes the master list of programs installed in DESQview. When you first install DESQview on your hard drive, the Open Window menu is created by the DESQview installation program, which scans your hard drive for application programs that match its built-in list.

All programs are listed in alphabetical order. Sometimes all the programs won't fit on the first Open Window menu screen. If this is the case, an option called More appears at the bottom of the menu to indicate that additional programs are listed on other menu pages. Press the **PgDn** key or select More with the mouse to view additional pages of programs.

See *Add a Program* for information about installing additional programs on the Open Window menu.

See Also *Add a Program, Big DOS, Close Window, Delete a Program, Switch Windows*

POSITION

- **PURPOSE** Places the active window in one of nine predesignated areas on your computer screen.

To Change the Position of the Active Window

1. Display the DESQview menu, as described in Part I, and select **Rearrange**.
2. Type the number corresponding to the window position you want.
3. The window will be moved, and the size will be changed as necessary to relocate it to the new position.

- **NOTES** DESQview uses nine predefined window positions, whose numbers are set by the initialization program when you install DESQview on your computer. All positions may be changed by running the Setup DESQview program.

Positions 1 and 2 split the screen in half horizontally, with one window at the top of the screen and the other at the bottom, as shown in Figure II.4. Position 3 locates a window that is smaller than the size of the screen directly in the center of the screen, as shown in Figure II.5.

Positions 4 and 5 split the screen in half vertically, with one window on the left and one on the right side of the screen, as shown in Figure II.6. Finally, positions 6, 7, 8, and 9 split the screen into quarters, each window taking up exactly one-quarter of the display, as shown in Figure II.7.

See Also *Move, Rearrange, Resize, Scroll, Setup DESQview, Specify Program Information, Zoom*

40   The DESQview Multitasking Environment

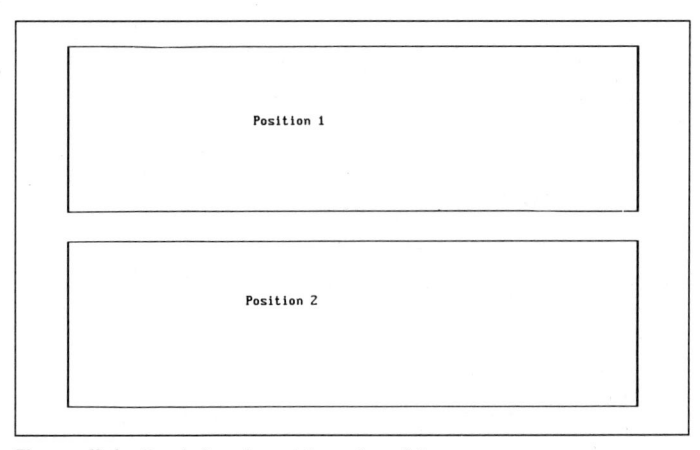

Figure II.4: Predefined positions 1 and 2

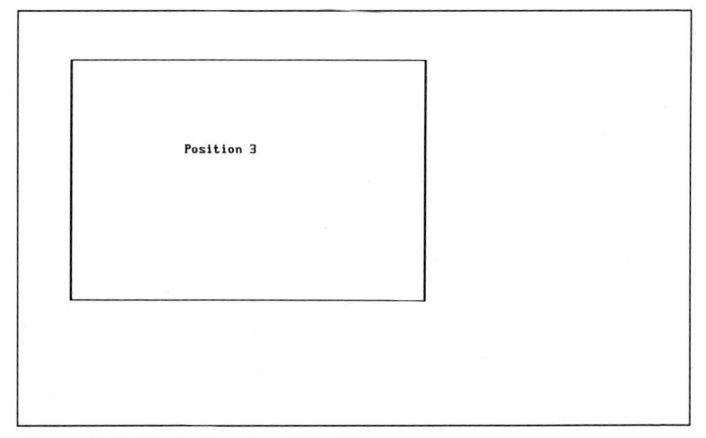

Figure II.5: Predefined position 3

Position **41**

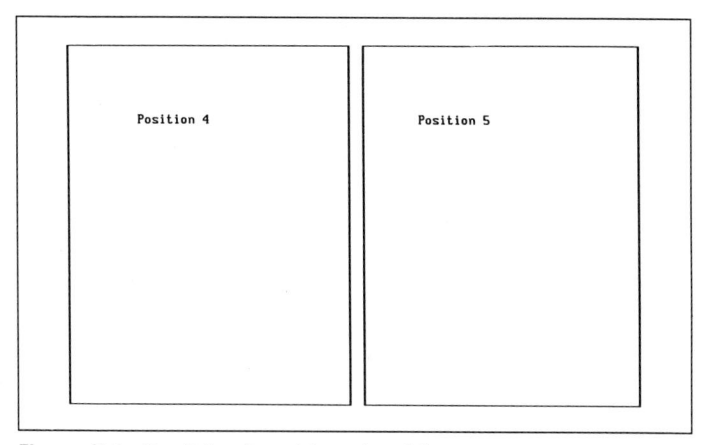

[Position 4 | Position 5]

Figure II.6: Predefined positions 4 and 5

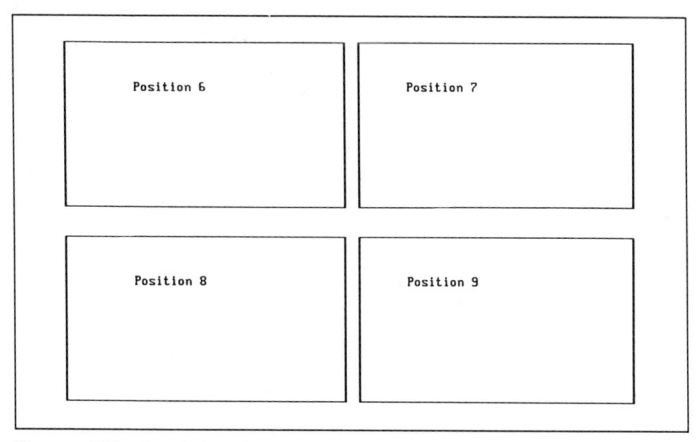

[Position 6 | Position 7]
[Position 8 | Position 9]

Figure II.7: Predefined positions 6, 7, 8, and 9

PUT ASIDE

- **PURPOSE** Hides the active window and suspends execution of your program. DESQview then swaps the program out to expanded memory or to disk. Once a window has been hidden, it can be redisplayed by using the Switch Windows command.

To Hide the Active Window and Suspend Execution of the Program

1. Display the DESQview menu, as described in Part I, and select **R**earrange.

2. Select **P**ut Aside from the Rearrange menu.

3. The message "Swapping..." appears while the window is being swapped out to expanded memory or to disk.

4. You will be returned to the DESQview menu, or you will find yourself in the window of the program you were working in previously.

See Also *Hide, Rearrange, Switch Windows, Types of Memory* (Part I)

QUIT DESQVIEW

- **PURPOSE** Exits the DESQview operating environment and returns control to DOS.

To Exit DESQview

1. Close each open window, making sure you save any important data you were working on. The only thing remaining on your screen should be the DESQview menu.

2. Select **Q**uit DESQview from the DESQview menu. A confirmation menu appears.

3. Press **Y** to confirm that you really want to exit DESQview. You will be returned to the DOS prompt.

• **NOTES** You don't always need to close all the windows before you exit DESQview, because DESQview will do it for you before it performs Quit. However, it's a good idea to make sure you save the data you were working on before Quit takes effect.

If any of the programs still running is configured so it can't be closed with the Close Window command, you won't be able to exit with Quit DESQview. To do so, first close down each such program by performing its exit command. WordPerfect and Lotus 1-2-3, release 3.1, are two examples.

See Also *Close Window*

REARRANGE

• **PURPOSE** Controls the appearance of the active window.

To Display the Rearrange Menu

1. Display the DESQview menu, as described in Part I, and select **R**earrange. The Rearrange menu will be displayed.

2. Select options from this menu just as you would from any other menu in DESQview.

• **NOTES** The commands found on the Rearrange menu (see Figure II.8) let you change the appearance of the active window. You can move it, change its size, scroll the contents of it, or change its position.

The DESQview Multitasking Environment

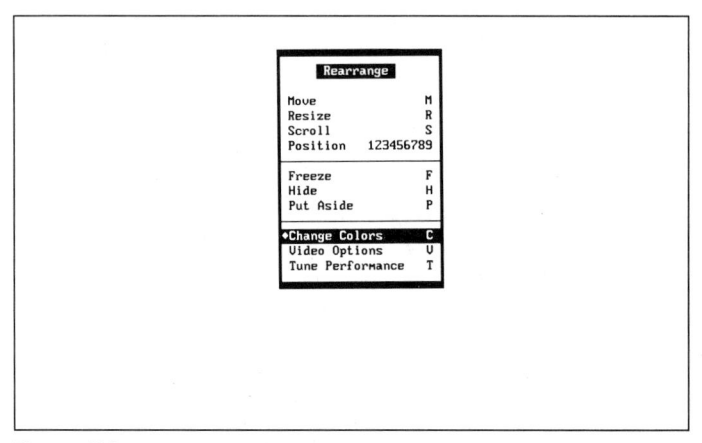

```
        ┌─────Rearrange─────┐
        │ Move            M │
        │ Resize          R │
        │ Scroll          S │
        │ Position 123456789│
        ├───────────────────┤
        │ Freeze          F │
        │ Hide            H │
        │ Put Aside       P │
        ├───────────────────┤
        │•Change Colors   C │
        │ Video Options   V │
        │ Tune Performance T│
        └───────────────────┘
```

Figure II.8: The Rearrange menu

Other menu options let you hide the active window, freeze the program running in it, or put it aside. You can also change the active window's colors.

Two other options give you more control over the active window. Video Options lets you select the current text and graphics video modes. A powerful option called Tune Performance lets you control, for the current session, the amount of time DESQview allocates to a foreground and to a background program, respectively.

Each of the Rearrange menu options is discussed as a separate entry in this book.

See Also *Change Colors, Freeze, Hide, Move, Position, Put Aside, Resize, Scroll, Tune Performance, Video Options*

RESIZE

• **PURPOSE** Changes the size of the active window. You can use either the arrow keys on your keyboard or the mouse connected to your computer.

To Change the Size of the Active Window Using the Keyboard

1. Display the DESQview menu, as described in Part I, and select **R**earrange.

2. Select **R**esize from the Rearrange menu.

3. Use the arrow keys to change the size of the current window: → and ↓ to expand, ← and ↑ to shrink.

To Change the Size of the Active Window Using the Mouse

1. Click the left mouse button on the lower frame of the active window. The Resize menu appears.

2. Move the mouse left and up or right and down. These actions will shrink or expand the window, using the upper-left corner as a pivot point.

3. Click the left mouse button again. Then select DONE from the Resize menu.

• **NOTES**   Sometimes it is easiest to use a combination of the keyboard and the mouse methods, leaving one hand on your mouse and the other hand on your keyboard.

See Also   *Move, Position, Rearrange, Scroll, Zoom*

SCISSORS

• **PURPOSE**   Allows you to transfer information between DESQview-specific programs. It works differently in each application that makes use of it. See the manual for the program you are using for specific keystroke information on how to use the command.

To exchange information between non-DESQview-specific DOS programs running in DESQview, see *Transfer*.

See Also *Mark, Transfer*

SCROLL

● **PURPOSE** Allows you to see a different part of a program's screen display when the program is running in a small window. A small window shows only a portion of the full-screen display, usually the area of the cursor's current location.

To Scroll to a Different View of a Program Using the Keyboard

1. Display the DESQview menu, as described in Part I, and select **R**earrange.

2. Select **S**croll from the Rearrange menu.

3. Use the arrow keys to scroll the active window to the view you want.

To Scroll to a Different View of a Program Using the Mouse

1. Click on the right side of the active window with the left mouse button.

2. Move the mouse until you have the view you want.

3. Double-click the left mouse button.

● **NOTES** Whether you scroll with the keyboard or the mouse, the window remains in the view you selected until you change it, even if you leave the window and return to it.

Setup DESQview **47**

See Also *Move, Position, Rearrange, Resize, Zoom*

SETUP DESQVIEW

- **PURPOSE** Allows you to configure DESQview. There are two methods to set up DESQview. Use the Simple Setup procedure when you are setting up DESQview for the first time after installing it on your system. Use the Advanced Setup procedure to "fine-tune" your system if you are an experienced user and you wish to take advantage of DESQview's more sophisticated features.

Once you have made any changes with the Setup program, you must exit DESQview and restart it for the changes to take effect.

To Configure DESQview Using the Simple Setup Procedure

1. Display the DESQview menu, as described in Part I, and select **O**pen Window.

2. Open a Big DOS window by selecting **B**ig **D**os from the list of programs.

3. Type **DVSETUP** from the DOS prompt in the Big DOS window. (If you have installed the Setup DESQview program on your Open Window menu, you may simply select it from the menu. See *Add a Program*.)

4. Press the **spacebar** to select the Simple Setup procedure. The setup program will examine your system's hardware configuration.

5. If you have a Color Graphics Adapter (CGA) board, an Enhanced Graphics Adapter (EGA) board, or a Video Graphics Array (VGA) board, you will be prompted, "Do you want DESQview to use color?" Answer **Y**es or **N**o

depending on the type of monitor connected to your display adapter board.

6. DESQview will ask if you have a mouse installed on your system. If you answer **Yes**, you are asked to specify the brand of the mouse you are using and the way the mouse is attached to your computer.

7. DESQview asks if you want to save the setup configuration. Press **Yes**, or press **No** to exit the Setup program without saving the setup configuration. The window will be closed and you will be returned to the program you were working in before you started the setup procedure, or to the DESQview menu if you were not in a program.

8. Exit DESQview and restart it to put your changes into effect.

To Configure DESQview Using the Advanced Setup Procedure

1. Display the DESQview menu, as described in Part I, and select **O**pen Window.

2. Open a Big Dos window by selecting **B**ig **D**OS from the list of programs.

3. Type **DVSETUP** from the DOS prompt in the Big DOS window. (If you have installed the Setup DESQview program on your Open Window menu, you may simply select it from the menu. See *Add a Program*.)

4. Press ↵ to start the Advanced Setup procedure. The Advanced Setup menu, shown in Figure II.9, will be displayed.

5. Select the option you want to configure from the list that completes the set of DESQview options you can modify. (See the Options section below for descriptions of the Advanced Setup options.)

6. Press ↵ to tell the program you are done, once you have the options set as you want them.

Setup DESQview 49

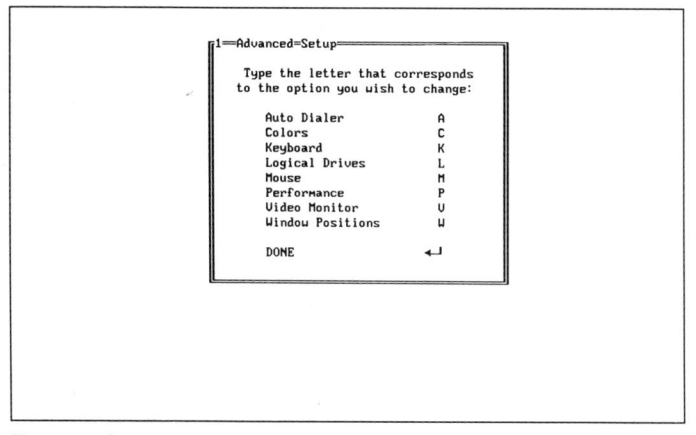

```
╔1═Advanced═Setup═════════════╗
║  Type the letter that corresponds
║  to the option you wish to change:
║
║      Auto Dialer            A
║      Colors                 C
║      Keyboard               K
║      Logical Drives         L
║      Mouse                  M
║      Performance            P
║      Video Monitor          V
║      Window Positions       W
║
║      DONE                   ↵
╚═════════════════════════════╝
```

Figure II.9: The Advanced Setup menu

7. Press ↵ again to store all the changes you have made and to quit the Setup program.

8. Exit DESQview and restart it to put your changes into effect.

Options

Auto Dialer lets you specify how DESQview will work with your modem in the following ways:

Dialer Port: You can select Port 1, 2, 3, or 4.

Dialer Baud Rate: You can select one of the available baud rates: 300, 600, 1200, 2400, 4800, or 9600.

Long Distance Access Codes: You can change the word used to describe the access code, as well as the digits used to access the code.

Change dialer protocol? The program is initially configured to use the Hayes Smartmodem protocol when communicating with your modem. If your modem is not Hayes-compatible, you can change the protocol by responding **Y**es to this option. A new menu will be displayed, which will allow you to change the *Prefix*—the commands to send before the

The DESQview Multitasking Environment

number; the *Postfix*—the commands to send after the number; and the *Hangup*—the commands to hang up your modem.

Colors lets you indicate whether you want DESQview to use color. If you do, you can specify the colors for programs as well as those for DESQview's own menus.

Keyboard lets you specify how DESQview will work with your keyboard in the following ways:

Do you want to use DESQview's Learn feature? If you want to use a different macro program, set this option to No. Otherwise, keep the Learn feature on.

Quoting Char for Learn: Enter the character you want to use to override a key's mapped meaning and perform the key's original action instead. The default is `. See *Learn*.

Memory Usage (in bytes): You can determine the size of each of the three global script buffers used by DESQview. The *DESQview Scripts* buffer is where all scripts learned on all DESQview menus are stored. The *Learn Scripts* buffer is the area of memory used to record a script while it's being learned. The *Playback Scripts* buffer is the area of memory used when you play back a script. Each buffer is initially set to 1024 bytes.

Maintain separate shift states for each window? This option is displayed when you are using DESQview 386. With it set to Yes, your keyboard can keep different shift states for each open window.

Change system keys? If you answer Yes to this command, Setup displays a new window and lets you change the keys used to invoke the DESQ, Learn, keyboard mouse, window-reboot, and system-reboot functions.

Logical Drives lets you define up to 16 logical drives. Use the **Tab** key to move among the drive letters A: through P:.

Mouse provides a way to tell DESQview the following information about the mouse you are using:

Mouse Type: Select among a keyboard mouse, a PC Mouse, a Microsoft mouse, a Logitech mouse, or a VisiOn mouse. (If you have a Logitech mouse, and you have MOUSE.COM or

MOUSE.SYS loaded, you can avoid potential problems in some programs by not selecting the Logitech mouse option.)

Mouse Port: Specify whether your mouse is connected by a bus or by communication port 1 or 2.

Left-handed mouse? If you answer Yes, Setup reverses the usage of the left and right mouse buttons so that the mouse is easier to use if you are left-handed.

Performance lets you customize the performance of DESQview to your personal needs in the following ways:

Task Processing Time: Specify the number of clock ticks to use when a task is in the foreground and when it is in the background.

Memory Usage: You can tell DESQview the amount of memory to use for a DESQview buffer (Common Memory) and for a DOS Buffer for EMS. Both are specified in kilobytes.

Optimize communications? Set this option to Yes unless you're running communications programs in DESQview and your computer freezes because of the optimization techniques used. If this is the case, set the option to No.

Allow swapping of programs? When DESQview needs more memory to run a program, it frees up memory by swapping the memory used by a background program out to expanded memory or to your disk drive. Normally, this is a desirable feature. Occasionally, however, if you have extremely limited memory, you may want to set this option to No.

Manage printer contention? If you are running background printing in several programs simultaneously, set this option to Yes, and DESQview will wait to print in one program until another is finished.

Video Monitor provides a means to configure DESQview in the following ways to use your video monitor to its full extent:

What display adapter do you have? Select among Monochrome, Color Graphics Adapter (CGA), Hercules, Enhanced Graphics Adapter (EGA), Video Graphics Array (VGA) or Micro Channel Graphics Adapter (MCGA), or another adapter. The display will show the current graphics driver DESQview is using.

Do you want text & graphics displayed at the same time? You can indicate whether you want DESQview to switch back to text mode or remain in graphics mode when you switch from a graphics program to a text program.

Does your display adapter require synchronized access? Answer **Yes** or **No**. If you get "snow" on your monitor, set this option to **Yes**.

Blank the screen after *xx* **minutes of inactivity**: Enter the number of minutes after which DESQview should automatically blank your screen when the system becomes idle.

Window Positions lets you change the nine predefined window positions used by DESQview when it opens a window and when you use the Position command on the Rearrange menu. For each position number, enter the number of the row and the column in which you want the window's upper-left corner to start, the height of the window in rows, and the width of the window in columns.

See Also *Add a Program, Auto Dialer, Change Colors, Learn, Memory Status, Position, Types of Memory* (Part I), *Video Options*

SPECIFY PROGRAM INFORMATION

- **PURPOSE** Gives you access to all the information DESQview has about a program. The information is divided into two screens. The first screen shows the standard program information, and the second one shows the advanced program information.

To View and Modify the Specify Program Information Screens

1. Display the DESQview menu, as described in Part I, and select **O**pen Window.

2. Select **C**hange a **P**rogram from the Open Window menu.

3. Select the program whose information you want to see. The standard program information screen appears.

4. Use the **Tab** key to move among the different option fields, each of which you may modify or leave as is. The fields are described in the Options section of this entry.

5. Press the **F1** key if you want to display the advanced options. Some of the advanced options listed behave differently in standard DESQview and in DESQview 386. Each is discussed in the Options section below.

6. Press ↵ to save the program information file to disk after you have filled out the option fields. If any fields are filled out incorrectly, DESQview will warn you and ask you to change the value in the associated field. Once you have done this, save the file again.

Options

The following standard options are found on the Specify Program Information screen, as seen in Figure II.10:

Program Name: Enter the program name you want to have appear on the Open Window menu.

Keys to Use on Open Menu: Type the two shortcut keys you want to use to open the program's window.

Memory Size: Specify the minimum amount of memory the program needs to run. If the program uses DOS, you must add 32K to the required amount of memory when you enter this value.

Program: This DOS command starts up the program. Usually, it will be the complete path name of the program, including the drive, the directory, and the file name with its extension.

54 The DESQview Multitasking Environment

```
┌Add=a=Program═══════════════════════════════════════════════════════════
│                         Specify Program Information
│ Program Name............:
│
│ Keys to Use on Open Menu:                            Memory Size (in K): 200
│
│ Program...: Enter pathname of program to run (C:\PROG\PROG.EXE)
│
│ Parameters: Enter command line parameters (/SWITCH)
│
│ Directory.:
│
│ Options:
│                    Writes text directly to screen.......: [Y]
│                    Displays graphics information........: [N]
│                    Virtualize text/graphics (Y,N,T).....: [Y]
│                    Uses serial ports (Y,N,1,2)..........: [N]
│                    Requires floppy diskette.............: [N]
│
│ Press F1 for advanced options              Press ↵ when you are DONE
```

Figure II.10: The Specify Program Information screen, standard options

Parameters: Use this field to specify any additional information which is usually passed on the DOS command line to the program. If the parameters are different each time you run the program, type a **?** as the last character, and DESQview will stop to let you type the command line each time the program's window is opened.

Directory: Specify the path on which you have stored the data files for the program. If you leave the field blank, DESQview assumes the program's data files are on the path from which you started DESQview.

Writes text directly to screen: Tell DESQview whether the program requires a full screen when it is running. With this option set to **Yes**, the program writes directly to the screen and requires the entire screen to run. With the option set to **No**, you can run the program in a window and move or resize the window.

Displays graphics information: If the program ever uses graphics mode, you must set this option to **Yes**.

Virtualize text/graphics: Set this option to **Yes** to tell DESQview to prevent the program from writing directly to the screen when it is running in the background. The program can then display its information in a window while it runs in the background. When you specify **Text**, DESQview will virtualize the program (allow you to run it in a small window) only

when it is in text mode. This option works only with
DESQview 386.

Uses serial ports: This option tells DESQview which serial
ports the program will use. If the program does not use the
serial ports, set it to **No**. This option works only with
DESQview 386.

Requires floppy disk: If the program you want to run is kept
on a floppy disk (for instance, if you are using DESQview on a
limited system), set this to **Yes**, and DESQview will remind
you to put the program disk in your floppy drive when the
window is first opened.

The following options are found on the Specify Program Information Advanced Options screen, as shown in Figure II.11:

System Memory: Specify the amount of memory, in addition
to what's needed for the program, to set aside for the system
when executing the program. The option is always set to 0 unless the program is DESQview-specific.

Maximum Program Memory Size: Specify the maximum
amount of memory to allocate to the program. Usually, you
leave this field empty and let DESQview manage memory for

```
┌Add=a=Program══════════════════════════════════════════════════
│           Specify Program Information Advanced Options
│
│  System Memory (in K).......:    0   Maximum Program Memory Size (in K)..:
│
│  Script Buffer Size.......: 1000     Maximum Expanded Memory Size (in K):
│
│  Text Pages: 1  Graphics Pages: 0   Initial Mode:     Interrupts: 00 to FF
│
│  Window Position:
│      Maximum Height:  25      Starting Height:        Starting Row...:
│      Maximum Width.:  80      Starting Width.:        Starting Column:
│                              Shared Program
│  Pathname..:
│  Data.....:
│
│  Close on exit (Y,N,blank)......: [ ]   Uses its own colors...............: [N]
│  Allow Close Window command.....: [Y]   Runs in background (Y,N,blank)...: [ ]
│  Uses math coprocessor..........: [Y]   Keyboard conflict (0-F)..........: [0]
│  Share CPU when foreground......: [Y]   Share EGA when foreground/zoomed.: [Y]
│  Can be swapped out (Y,N,blank).: [ ]   Protection level (0-3)...........: [0]
│
│     Press F1 for standard options          Press ◄┘ when you are DONE
```

Figure II.11: The Specify Program Information Advanced
Options screen

you. However, if you want the program to access only a certain amount of memory, you should enter that amount here.

Script Buffer Size: Enter the amount of memory to set aside for program script buffers when using the Learn feature of DESQview. The default is 1024 bytes, which will accommodate up to about 20 scripts.

Maximum Expanded Memory Size: Use this option to limit the amount of expanded memory the program can use for itself. Some programs grab as much expanded memory as possible, even if they don't use it all. The result when you're using DESQview is deteriorated system performance, because DESQview could use the memory itself.

Text Pages: Specify the number of pages of memory to set aside for programs operating in text mode. Most programs use only one page of text memory.

Graphics Pages: Specify the number of pages to set aside for the program when it runs in graphics mode. If the program doesn't use graphics, don't enter anything in this field.

Initial Mode: Specify the hardware video mode that DESQview should switch to when the program is first started. This is used mainly by programmers. You can leave the field empty without any harm.

Interrupts: This option tells DESQview the range of interrupts to save. Usually the number is from 00 hex to FF hex. This is another option used mostly by programmers.

Maximum Height: Specify the greatest possible height of the program's window. The default is 25.

Maximum Width: Specify the greatest possible width of the program's window. The default is 80.

Starting Height: Indicate the initial height on the screen of the program's window.

Starting Width: Indicate the initial width on the screen of the program's window.

Starting Row: Specify the position of the first row relative to the upper-left corner of the program's window.

Starting Column: Specify the position of the first column relative to the upper-left corner of the program's window.

Specify Program Information 57

Shared Program Pathname: Specify a DOS file containing a DESQview-specific program to be shared with this program. Leave this field empty unless you have a program that instructs you to enter information in it.

Shared Program Data: Enter the file name of the data to be sent to the shared program. This option is used for DESQview-specific programs. Leave this field empty unless you have a program that instructs you to enter information in it.

Close on exit (Y, N, blank): This option tells DESQview whether to perform the Close Window command automatically when the program is exited in a normal fashion. If you leave the field blank, DESQview makes the decision.

Uses its own colors: Tell DESQview whether to use the program's own colors or to assign a set of colors when the program is opened. Set this option to Yes when you want to use the program's own predefined colors.

Allow Close Window command: With this option set to Yes, you may close the window at any time by selecting Close Window from the DESQview menu. When the option is set to No, the only way to close a window is by exiting the program.

Runs in background (Y, N, blank): This option tells DESQview whether to allow the program to run in the background while another program is running in the foreground. If you leave the field blank, DESQview makes the best decision as it is running.

Uses math coprocessor: Specify that DESQview should allocate additional memory for the information needed to manage the math coprocessor when running the program.

Keyboard conflict: Indicate how DESQview is to manage the keyboard buffer for the program. Most programs run with this option set to 0, which is the default.

Share CPU when foreground: Tell DESQview whether to allow other programs to run in the background when this program is executing in the foreground.

Share EGA when foreground/zoomed: Set this option to Yes to allow other EGA graphics programs to run in the background. If you enter No, DESQview will freeze EGA programs running in the background when this program is zoomed to a full-screen display.

58 The DESQview Multitasking Environment

Can be swapped out (Y, N, blank): With this option set to Yes, the program can be swapped out of memory to expanded memory or to disk when DESQview needs memory for another program. Most programs can run with this option set to Yes. The only exceptions are communication programs such as Crosstalk or ProComm Plus.

Protection level: Indicate whether you want to protect the program against "ill-behaved" programs. The field can be filled in with values from 0 through 3. Selecting 0 tells DESQview not to provide special protection. The higher the number you set, the more levels of protection you specify. Setting a protection level results in some performance loss on your system. This option works in conjunction with QEMM-386.

- **NOTES** Every program that DESQview has listed on its Open Window menu is set up to run in the DESQview operating environment. In order for DESQview to execute advanced features, such as running multiple programs in windows and multitasking, it must have additional information about the programs.

The information you enter is saved in a program information file. The name of the file is a combination of the letters you assign to access the program from the Open Window menu and an extension. The result is a file name that looks like "*xx*-PIF.DVP," where *xx* is the key combination you assigned to open the program.

Quarterdeck Office Systems includes all the standard information needed to run over 120 programs, so you can start working in DESQview quickly, without first having to specify program information. See *Add a Program* for more information.

DESQview 386 needs to have more information about a program than does standard DESQview, so it can make use of the powerful features of the 80386 microprocessor. When you're filling out the program information screens, it is helpful to have the program's documentation handy. It is also useful to have some knowledge about how the program operates.

See Also *Add a Program, Change a Program, Memory Status, Position, Tune Performance, Types of Memory* (Part I), *"Well-behaved" and "Ill-behaved" Programs* (Part I)

SWITCH WINDOWS

- **PURPOSE** Allows you to change the active window from the one you are presently working in to another window that is open on your screen.

To Switch Windows with the Keyboard

1. Display the DESQview menu, as described in Part I, and select Switch Windows. A list of the currently open windows will be displayed.

2. Type the number corresponding to the window you want to switch to.

Shortcut Immediately after you have displayed the DESQview menu, type the number corresponding to the window you want to open, without going through the Switch Windows screen.

To Switch Windows with a Mouse

1. Be sure that the window you want to make the active window is open and visible on the screen.

2. Move the diamond-shaped mouse cursor into the window you want to switch to, and click the left mouse button.

- **NOTES** Use the Switch Windows menu when you want to see a list of all the windows currently open on your screen.

Whether you select a window number with the keyboard or click in a window with a mouse, the frame of the window you have switched to changes to a double line to signify that it has become the active window.

See Also *Close Window, Hide, Open Window, Put Aside, Transfer*

60 The DESQview Multitasking Environment

TRANSFER

- **PURPOSE** Used in conjunction with the Mark command to cut and paste information from the screen of a non-DESQview-specific program to the screen of any other program.

To Transfer Information from One Program to Another

1. Make sure that both the programs you want to transfer information between are open and available on the Switch Windows menu. Start in the window of the program which you want to copy information from.

2. Display the DESQview menu, as described in Part I, and select **M**ark. The Mark menu will be displayed.

3. Use the arrow keys or the mouse to position the cursor at the upper-left corner of the block of information you want to transfer. Select Mark **B**egin from the Mark menu.

4. Move the cursor to the lower-right corner of the block of information you want to transfer. Select Mark **E**nd from the Mark menu. The information will be captured by DESQview and saved in a special buffer.

5. Activate the window of the destination program (see *Switch Windows*), and move the cursor to the location where you want the information transferred.

6. Display the DESQview menu, and select **T**ransfer.

7. Press ↵ or **T**, and the information will be transferred to the destination program.

- **NOTES** The DESQview Transfer command copies information to a program just as if you had typed it in from the keyboard. The maximum amount of information the Mark command allows you to transfer is the amount that can fit on one screen at a single time. If you are using a DESQview-specific program, you may be able to use the Scissors command to copy more than one screen of data at a time.

You can transfer information from one program to two or more other programs which are all open simultaneously. You must repeat Steps 5 through 7 for each additional program.

If you are moving lots of information between programs and the task becomes repetitive, it would be wise to create a DESQview script to automate the process. See the *Learn* entry.

See Also   *Learn, Mark, Scissors, Switch Windows*

TUNE PERFORMANCE

- **PURPOSE**   Allows you to adjust certain features of DESQview's performance in a program during your current DESQview session.

To Control Program-Specific Options

1. Display the DESQview menu, as described in Part I, and select **R**earrange.

2. Select **T**une Performance from the Rearrange menu. The Tune Performance menu, shown in Figure II.12, will be displayed.

3. Use the **Tab** key to move among the different option fields, described in the Options section of this entry.

4. If your mouse has stopped responding, use the Revive Mouse command (press the **F1** key) on the menu to reset it.

5. Press ↵ to make your changes take effect immediately, or press **Esc** to cancel all the changes you made.

62 The DESQview Multitasking Environment

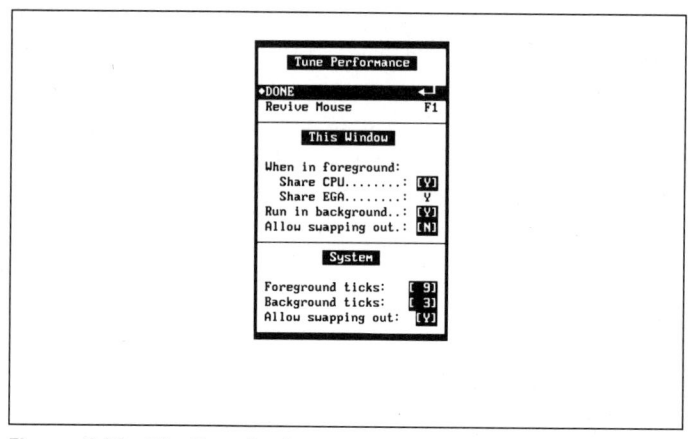

Figure II.12: The Tune Performance menu

Options

When in foreground Share CPU tells DESQview whether to allow other programs to run in the background while the current program runs in the foreground.

When in foreground Share EGA instructs DESQview whether to allow other EGA graphics programs to run in the background. Enter **No** and DESQview will freeze EGA programs running in the background if the current program is in EGA graphics mode and is zoomed to full screen.

Run in background specifies whether the current program can run in the background when you switch to another window. Normally, you leave this field empty, allowing DESQview to decide when the program will run in the background and when it won't.

Allow swapping out (This Window) controls whether DESQview can swap this program's window to expanded memory or to disk when it needs memory to run another program. Set this option to **No** if you want the program always available instantly.

Foreground ticks lets you change the number of clock ticks (the default is 9) that DESQview gives to your programs when they are running.

Video Options 63

Background ticks lets you change the number of clock ticks (the default is 3) that DESQview gives to each background program running. These two options are useful when you're multitasking to control which application DESQview gives the most attention to.

Allow swapping out (System) tells DESQview whether or not to swap the program to expanded memory or to disk when it needs more memory than is available to run programs. This is different from the above option because this one applies to the whole system rather than to a window.

● **NOTES** The changes you make to options using the Tune Performance menu are temporary, staying in effect only until you change them again or until you quit DESQview.

You can make the changes permanent, however, by selecting the Change a Program option from the Open Window menu and resetting the corresponding information found in the program's information file.

See Also *Change a Program, Rearrange, Specify Program Information*

VIDEO OPTIONS

● **PURPOSE** Allows you to change text and graphics video modes. Use it to control the number of lines displayed on the screen at any time.

To Change the Current Video Mode

1. Display the DESQview menu, as described in Part I, and select **R**earrange.
2. Select **V**ideo Options from the Rearrange menu.

64 The DESQview Multitasking Environment

3. Type the number corresponding to the mode you want to use, or position the mouse over your selection and click the left mouse button.

4. Select DONE to complete your selection.

• **NOTES** To use this command, you must have either an Enhanced Graphics Adapter (EGA), a Video Graphics Array (VGA), a Micro Channel Graphics Adapter (MCGA), a Hercules, or a Micro Display Systems Genius Display board. The type of monitor and adapter you are using will limit the modes you can use.

Sometimes DESQview changes the video mode to one which is best suited to display the programs currently being executed. In this case, DESQview will ignore the setting of the Video Options menu.

See Also *Rearrange, Setup DESQview*

ZOOM

• **PURPOSE** Allows you to enlarge a small window to full-screen size and to shrink it back to its original size and position when selected again.

To Display the Active Window in a Full Screen

1. Display the DESQview menu, as described in Part I.

2. Select Zoom. The window will be enlarged to take up the whole screen.

To Restore a Zoomed Window to Its Previous Size

1. Display the DESQview menu, as described in Part I.

2. Select Zoom. The window will be returned to its previous size and position.

● **NOTES** Not all programs can be run in a small window. If DESQview beeps when you select the Zoom option, this window's size cannot be changed.

See Also *Move, Position, Resize, Scroll*

Part III

QEMM, the Quarterdeck Expanded Memory Manager

QEMM-386, the Quarterdeck Expanded Memory Manager, is a software control program used to oversee the use of memory in your computer. It is actually made up of several programs. This part of the book explains in full detail each of QEMM's programs. The parameters that control each program are given, along with hints for using the programs. Most of the information in this section is required only by the advanced user—most people will just glance through the section to get an idea of what the QEMM programs are capable of doing.

As discussed under *Concepts and Terminology* in Part I, there are three types of memory—conventional, expanded, and extended—in DOS-based computers, and each is accessed in different ways. QEMM uses all three types, allocating memory to DOS, TSRs (terminate-and-stay-resident programs), and application programs as efficiently as possible. It supports all memory drivers for each type of memory. In addition, the QEMM package contains programs that can map certain parts of DOS and TSRs into expanded or extended memory to give the user additional conventional memory to use for running programs.

The QEMM program that does the main memory management is a device driver called QEMM386.SYS. It is installed in your CONFIG.SYS configuration file and is loaded automatically the first time you start your computer after installing DESQview.

QEMM.COM is used to turn memory management on and off and to report status information about the device driver. The OPTIMIZE program will scan your AUTOEXEC.BAT and CONFIG.SYS files and configure QEMM to make optimum use of your system memory to run the programs you use most often.

Two programs, called LOADHI.COM and LOADHI.SYS, enable you to load TSR programs, device drivers, and DOS resources into regions of memory in high RAM, giving you more conventional memory to run your programs. Four programs, called the DOS resources, let you manage the data structures used by DOS. They are commonly used with LOADHI and are named after the DOS resources they manage. Their names are BUFFERS.COM, FCBS.COM,FILES.COM, and LASTDRIVE.COM.

A program called VIDRAM.COM lets you increase your conventional memory by letting DOS use the memory normally reserved for graphics on your EGA or VGA video adapter card. If you use graphics all the time, you can't use VIDRAM.COM, but if you don't use graphics applications, you can gain up to an additional 96K of memory by using this program.

OPTIMIZE

The OPTIMIZE program is executed automatically when you first install QEMM. It scans your computer's configuration files to find device drivers, TSRs, and DOS resources that can be put in the high memory area. It then modifies your AUTOEXEC.BAT and CONFIG.SYS files to work well with these programs.

You must reboot your computer twice to complete the OPTIMIZE procedure. Once this is done, OPTIMIZE will report how much memory has been freed up. The amount freed up will depend upon how efficiently your computer's memory was being used before you ran OPTIMIZE.

After installing it initially, you should run OPTIMIZE periodically so it can sense any new programs that may be on your system. In addition, if you change the configuration of your computer, you should run the program again so the computer will operate at its optimum.

QEMM386.SYS

QEMM386.SYS is automatically installed in the CONFIG.SYS configuration file of your computer when you run the INSTALL program. The parameters described in the following sections all control or limit the way QEMM386.SYS works. To use one or more of them, add their names to the QEMM line you create in your CONFIG.SYS file. Before editing, the line looks like this:

DEVICE=QEMM386.SYS

You can have only one such line in your CONFIG.SYS file, and it can include as many parameters as will fit on one line. Parameters must be separated by spaces, but they may not contain spaces.

Finally, after you make any changes to your CONFIG.SYS file, it is imperative that you reboot your system. New parameters take effect only when you start your computer or when you reboot it.

QEMM386.SYS ?

- **PURPOSE** Displays a brief list of all parameters available in the QEMM386.SYS program.

- **SYNTAX**

    DEVICE=QEMM386.SYS ?

- **NOTE** If you specify the ? parameter, any other parameters on the line will be ignored.

- **EXAMPLE** Include the following line in your CONFIG.SYS file, and whenever you start your computer, a list of QEMM386.SYS parameters will appear on the screen:

    DEVICE=QEMM386.SYS ?

See Also   *QEMM386.SYS HELP*

QEMM386.SYS ADAPTERRAM

- **PURPOSE** Marks an area of RAM as being mapped to an adapter in a specific range of memory. Specify in hexadecimal notation the beginning and ending addresses of the memory area to be marked.

- **SYNTAX**

    DEVICE=QEMM386.SYS ARAM=*xxxx-yyyy*

- **NOTES** This parameter is usually used to identify a network adapter board. Usually, QEMM automatically finds memory areas occupied by adapters. However, it cannot recognize the presence of certain adapters, so you must specify their location.

- **EXAMPLE** Include the following line in your CONFIG.SYS file to identify an area of RAM from CC00 hex to CFFF hex as RAM which is on a separate adapter card, to tell QEMM to fill in areas of high memory which have no RAM or ROM mapped to them and not to provide expanded memory services, and to set up a 64K disk buffer for a SCSI hard drive:

    DEVICE=QEMM386.SYS ARAM=CC00-CFFF RAM NOEMS DB=64

See Also *QEMM386.SYS ADAPTERROM, QEMM386.SYS DISK-BUF, QEMM386.SYS EXCLUDE, QEMM386.SYS NOEMS, QEMM-386.SYS RAM*

QEMM386.SYS ADAPTERROM

- **PURPOSE** Marks an area of ROM as being mapped to a separate adapter in a specific range of memory. Specify in hexadecimal notation the beginning and ending addresses of the memory area to be marked.

- **SYNTAX**

    DEVICE=QEMM386.SYS AROM=*xxxx-yyyy*

- **NOTES** Similar to the ADAPTERRAM parameter, this one is used to identify special adapter boards as having ROM. QEMM usually automatically finds memory areas occupied by adapters, but it cannot recognize the presence of certain adapters, so you must specify their location.

- **EXAMPLE** Include the following line in your CONFIG.SYS file to specify that the area of ROM from B800 hex to BFFF hex is on a separate adapter card, to tell QEMM not to trap the 8042 port, to set the number of handles to 45, and to tell QEMM not to use shadow RAM:

    DEVICE=QEMM386.SYS AROM=B800-BFFF IA HA=45 NOSH

See Also   *QEMM386.SYS ADAPTERRAM, QEMM386.SYS EXCLUDE, QEMM386.SYS HANDLES, QEMM386.SYS IGNOREA20, QEMM386.SYS NOSHADOWRAM*

QEMM386.SYS AUTO

- **PURPOSE**   Used to tell QEMM to turn itself on only when a program needs expanded memory. The AUTO mode is used by default in QEMM unless you specify the ON or OFF parameter explicitly.

- **SYNTAX**

    DEVICE=QEMM386.SYS AU

- **EXAMPLE**   Include the following line in your CONFIG.SYS file to tell QEMM to turn itself on only when a program needs expanded memory, to identify an area of RAM from CC00 hex to CFFF hex as RAM that is on a separate adapter card, and to set the maximum length of a direct memory access transfer to 57K:

    DEVICE=QEMM386.SYS AU ARAM=CC00-CFFF DM=57

See Also   *QEMM386.SYS ADAPTERRAM, QEMM386.SYS DMA, QEMM386.SYS OFF, QEMM386.SYS ON*

QEMM386.SYS COMPAQ386S

- **PURPOSE**   Identifies the computer with which you are using QEMM as a Compaq 386S. You need to use this switch only if the setup program you are using on your Compaq 386S is previous to version 6.02.

- **SYNTAX**

    DEVICE=QEMM386.SYS C386S

QEMM386.SYS

- **EXAMPLE** Include the following line in your CONFIG.SYS file to tell QEMM that it is being executed on a Compaq 386S computer and that it should not look for top memory, to set the amount of extended memory QEMM should use to 64K, and to tell QEMM not to halt the display when a message appears on the screen:

DEVICE=QEMM386.SYS C386S NT EXT=64 NOPE

See Also *QEMM386.SYS COMPAQEGAROM, QEMM386.SYS COMPAQHALFROM, QEMM386.SYS COMPAQROMMEMORY, QEMM386.SYS EXTMEM, QEMM386.SYS NOCOMPAQFEATURES, QEMM386.SYS NOPAUSEONERROR, QEMM386.SYS NOTOPMEMORY*

QEMM386.SYS COMPAQEGAROM

- **PURPOSE** Relocates the video ROM in a Compaq computer to increase the amount of high memory. When a Compaq computer starts up, it automatically copies the slow video ROM to fast memory at a different address. By using the COMPAQEGAROM switch, you can prevent this from occurring. As a result, more memory will be available for your programs to use.

- **SYNTAX**

DEVICE=QEMM386.SYS CER

- **EXAMPLE** Inlcude the following line in your CONFIG.SYS file to relocate the video ROM in a Compaq computer, to tell QEMM that it's being used with PC-DOS 4.00 with the /X instruction, to set the number of alternate maps available to 79, and to tell QEMM not to map a reboot page of system ROM:

DEVICE=QEMM386.SYS CER D4 MAPS=79 NR

See Also *QEMM386.SYS DOS4, QEMM386.SYS MAPS, QEMM386.SYS NOCOMPAQFEATURES, QEMM386.SYS NOROM*

QEMM386.SYS COMPAQHALFROM

- **PURPOSE** Cuts a Compaq computer's system ROM in half. On most Compaq computers, system ROM consists of two parts, which are mapped into separate areas. These areas include redundant information. Specify this parameter to use just one of the areas of ROM, thereby making better use of your memory.

- **SYNTAX**

    DEVICE=QEMM386.SYS CHR

- **EXAMPLE** Include the following line in your CONFIG.SYS file to prevent two different mappings of the same area of memory on your Compaq computer, to set the disk buffer size to 164K when using a SCSI hard drive, to tell QEMM that it's being used with a version of DESQview prior to 2.01 and that the method used to determine the amount of extended memory is nonstandard:

    DEVICE=QEMM386.SYS CHR DB=164 ODV UX

See Also *QEMM386.SYS DISKBUF, QEMM386.SYS NOCOMPAQ-FEATURES, QEMM386.SYS OLDDV, QEMM386.SYS UNUSUALEXT*

QEMM386.SYS COMPAQROMMEMORY

- **PURPOSE** Tells QEMM to use the 128K of memory reserved on Compaq Deskpro 386 computers to speed up their system ROM. By using this parameter, you will speed up the system ROM in your computer and make this 128K of high memory available to other programs.

- **SYNTAX**

    DEVICE=QEMM386.SYS CRM

- **EXAMPLE** Include the following line in your CONFIG.SYS file to free up an additional 128K of memory on your Compaq computer, to specify a page frame address at D000 hex, to set 128K as the minimum amount of memory that a program using the XMS high memory area can request, and to tell QEMM to pause when outputting messages to the screen:

DEVICE=QEMM386.SYS CRM FR=D000 HMAMIN=128 PAUSE

See Also *QEMM386.SYS FRAME, QEMM386.SYS HMAMIN, QEMM386.SYS NOCOMPAQFEATURES, QEMM386.SYS PAUSE*

QEMM386.SYS DISKBUF

- **PURPOSE** Lets you specify the size of the disk buffer. Use it only if you have a SCSI hard drive. Because of the way SCSI hard drives access memory, QEMM's normal direct memory access (DMA) buffering method is not adequate. Use this parameter to specify the size of the buffer to use. The number is always in kilobytes.

- **SYNTAX**

DEVICE=QEMM386.SYS DB=*xx*

- **NOTES** SCSI, or Small Computer System Interface, is one standard method for connecting a hard drive to a PC.

- **EXAMPLE** Include the following line in your CONFIG.SYS file to set up a 16K buffer for your SCSI hard drive, to tell QEMM to switch on only when a program requires memory management services, to specify that all the system ROM BIOS should be copied to RAM and then mapped into its original location in ROM, and to tell QEMM that you're using it with PC-DOS 4.00 with the /X instruction:

DEVICE=QEMM386.SYS DB=16 AU ROM=F000-FFFF D4

See Also *QEMM386.SYS AUTO, QEMM386.SYS DOS4, QEMM-386.SYS ROM*

QEMM386.SYS DMA

- **PURPOSE**   Specifies the maximum length of a direct memory access (DMA) transfer. The number used must be in the range 12K to 128K.

- **SYNTAX**

    DEVICE=QEMM386.SYS DM=*xxx*

- **EXAMPLE**   Include the following line in your CONFIG.SYS file to set the maximum length of a direct memory access transfer to 49K, to tell QEMM to switch on only when a program requires memory management services, to set the number of handles to 128, and to disable all Compaq features:

    DEVICE=QEMM386.SYS DM=49 AU HA=128 NCF

See Also   *QEMM386.SYS AUTO, QEMM386.SYS HANDLES, QEMM386.SYS LOCKDMA, QEMM386.SYS NOCOMPAQFEATURES*

QEMM386.SYS DOS4

- **PURPOSE**   Alters EMS page ordering so that QEMM will operate correctly when you're using PC-DOS version 4.00 with the /X command, which does not access memory in strict accordance with the EMS specifications.

- **SYNTAX**

    DEVICE=QEMM386.SYS D4

- **EXAMPLE**   Include the following line in your CONFIG.SYS file to tell QEMM you are using PC-DOS 4.00 with the /X parameter, to disable all Compaq features, and to tell QEMM not to look for top memory and that you're working on a computer with a nonstandard 8042 keyboard controller:

    DEVICE=QEMM386.SYS D4 NCF NT U8

QEMM386.SYS EMBMEM

See Also *QEMM386.SYS NOCOMPAQFEATURES, QEMM-386.SYS NOTOPMEMORY, QEMM386.SYS UNUSUAL8042*

QEMM386.SYS EMBMEM

- **PURPOSE** Sets the maximum amount of memory, defined in kilobytes, that a program which uses the XMS extended memory specification will see as available. The default is 12,288K (12 megabytes).

- **SYNTAX**

   DEVICE=QEMM386.SYS EMB=*xxxxx*

- **EXAMPLE** Include the following line in your CONFIG.SYS file to set the maximum amount of XMS extended memory to 640K:

   DEVICE=QEMM386.SYS EMB=640

See Also *QEMM386.SYS NOXMS*

QEMM386.SYS EXCLUDE

- **PURPOSE** Lets you specify, in a multiple of 4K, a range in the first megabyte of memory that should be unmappable and should not be controlled by QEMM. You need to specify an excluded region of memory only if QEMM can't detect it. Specify in hexadecimal notation the beginning and ending addresses of the memory you want to exclude. You can exclude multiple ranges of memory by inserting the parameter more than once.

- **SYNTAX**

   DEVICE=QEMM386.SYS X=*xxxx-yyyy*

- **EXAMPLE** Include the following line in your CONFIG.SYS file to exclude the memory in the ranges C100 hex to C1FF hex and

F000 hex to F5FF hex and to tell QEMM to pause when outputting messages to the screen:

DEVICE=QEMM386.SYS X=C100-C1FF X=F000-F5FF PAUSE

See Also   *QEMM386.SYS ADAPTERRAM, QEMM386.SYS ADAPTERROM, QEMM386.SYS INCLUDE, QEMM386.SYS PAUSE*

QEMM386.SYS EXTMEM

- **PURPOSE**   Reserves a block of extended memory, which won't be used by QEMM, for use by another program. Specify the number in kilobytes from 1 to 31,744.

- **SYNTAX**

   DEVICE=QEMM386.SYS EXT=*xxxxx*

- **NOTES**   If you use a RAM disk like the one that comes with DOS, you should use this parameter to free the extended memory for your RAM disk.

- **EXAMPLE**   Include the following line in your CONFIG.SYS file to leave at least 832K of memory free for a RAM disk, to tell QEMM to fill in areas of high memory that don't have RAM or ROM mapped to them, to disable automatic detection of unused addresses in ROM, and to tell QEMM not to sort memory by its speed:

   DEVICE=QEMM386.SYS EXT=832 RAM NRH NS

See Also   *QEMM386.SYS MEMORY, QEMM386.SYS NOROMHOLES, QEMM386.SYS NOSORT, QEMM386.SYS RAM*

QEMM386.SYS FORCEEMS

- **PURPOSE**   Instructs QEMM to allow EMS expanded memory requests to be acknowledged. Use this parameter only if you have used the FRAMELENGTH parameter with a value less than 4. FORCEEMS will then allow programs to have limited access to expanded memory, even without a full page frame.

- **SYNTAX**

    DEVICE=QEMM386.SYS FEMS

- **EXAMPLE**   Include the following line in your CONFIG.SYS file to allow EMS memory requests to be honored even though your page frame contains only 3 pages:

    DEVICE=QEMM386.SYS FEMS FL=3

See Also   *QEMM386.SYS FRAMELENGTH*

QEMM386.SYS FRAME

- **PURPOSE**   Specifies the beginning page frame address of the 64K segment through which EMS memory is mapped. Use it only when accessing expanded memory. If you don't specify the frame parameter, QEMM chooses the value according to the way your hardware is set up. To turn EMS memory management off, set **FR=NONE**. Only in very rare instances would you use the FRAME parameter.

- **SYNTAX**

    DEVICE=QEMM386.SYS FR=*xxxx*

- **EXAMPLE**   Include the following line in your CONFIG.SYS file to set the page frame address to A000 hex if you have a monochrome video adapter and QEMM can't find a frame area, to tell QEMM you're working with a version of DESQview prior to 2.01, to instruct QEMM not to be an extended memory manager and to fill in areas of high memory that have no RAM or ROM mapped to them, and to tell QEMM not to use shadow RAM:

    DEVICE=QEMM386.SYS FR=A000 ODV NOXMS RAM NOSH

See Also   *QEMM386.SYS FRAMELENGTH, QEMM386.SYS NO-SHADOWRAM, QEMM386.SYS NOXMS, QEMM386.SYS OLDDV, QEMM386.SYS RAM*

QEMM386.SYS FRAMELENGTH

- **PURPOSE**   Tells QEMM to assume a page frame containing a specified number of pages. You can set the number from 0 to 4. Setting it to 0 is the same as not having a page frame at all. Normally, the frame length is set by the EMS memory manager, with four page frames as standard.

- **SYNTAX**

    DEVICE=QEMM386.SYS FL=*x*

- **EXAMPLE**   Include the following line in your CONFIG.SYS file to specify 2 page frames for EMS memory and to tell QEMM to honor EMS memory requests:

    DEVICE=QEMM386.SYS FL=2 FEMS

See Also   *QEMM386.SYS FORCEEMS, QEMM386.SYS FRAME*

QEMM386.SYS HANDLES

- **PURPOSE**   Specifies the number of "handles," or names, that QEMM should use to access expanded memory. Every program that uses expanded memory requires at least one handle—the default is 64. The value you specify is a decimal number from 16 to 255. Each handle requires 28 bytes of memory overhead for DOS to keep track of it.

- **SYNTAX**

    DEVICE=QEMM386.SYS HA=*xxx*

- **EXAMPLE**   Include the following line in your CONFIG.SYS file to set the number of expanded memory handles to 128, to tell QEMM to copy the ROM BIOS area to RAM and then map it to its original location in ROM, and to tell QEMM that you have an adapter board installed in the range C000 hex through CFFF hex:

    DEVICE=QEMM386.SYS HA=128 ROM=F000-FFFF
    AROM=CC00-CFFF

See Also   *QEMM386.SYS ADAPTERROM, QEMM386.SYS ROM*

QEMM386.SYS HELP

- **PURPOSE**   Displays a list of all QEMM386.SYS parameters with a description of each one.

- **SYNTAX**

    DEVICE=QEMM386.SYS HELP

- **NOTES**   This parameter is helpful if you need to remind yourself what a certain parameter does. When you use HELP, all other parameters on the line are ignored.

- **EXAMPLE**   Include the following line in your CONFIG.SYS file to list all descriptions of the parameters you can use with QEMM386.SYS:

    DEVICE=QEMM386.SYS HELP

See Also   *QEMM386.SYS ?*

QEMM386.SYS HMAMIN

- **PURPOSE**   Sets the minimum amount of memory required for a program to access the XMS high memory area (HMA). Although several programs may want to use the HMA, the only program that can use it is the one requesting the amount of memory specified with this parameter. The number specified on the command line is in kilobytes.

- **SYNTAX**

    DEVICE=QEMM386.SYS HMAMIN=*xx*

- **EXAMPLE**   Include the following line in your CONFIG.SYS file to allow a program that requests at least 55K of memory to have access to the HMA high memory area, to turn QEMM on as a memory manager, and to tell QEMM not to provide expanded memory services and not to use shadow RAM:

    DEVICE=QEMM386.SYS HMAMIN=55 ON NOEMS NOSH

See Also   *QEMM386.SYS NOEMS, QEMM386.SYS NOSHADOWRAM, QEMM386.SYS ON*

QEMM386.SYS IGNOREA20

- **PURPOSE**   Tells QEMM not to trap the 8042 port. Some programs try to access this port to specify to QEMM that a program can use a driver called HIMEM.SYS. Since QEMM can access extended memory, there is no need to use HIMEM.SYS. It is rare that you would need to use this parameter.

- **SYNTAX**

    DEVICE=QEMM386.SYS IA

- **EXAMPLE**   Include the following line in your CONFIG.SYS file to tell QEMM to disable support of HIMEM.SYS, not to sort memory by its speed, to pause when outputting messages to the screen, and to set the maximum length of a direct memory access transfer to 45K:

    DEVICE=QEMM386.SYS IA NS PAUSE DM=45

See Also   *QEMM386.SYS DMA, QEMM386.SYS NOSORT, QEMM-386.SYS PAUSE*

QEMM386.SYS INCLUDE

- **PURPOSE**   Lets you specify a range of memory in a multiple of 4K that QEMM should consider mappable. That range will then be controlled by QEMM. Specify in hexadecimal notation the beginning and ending addresses of the memory to be included.

- **SYNTAX**

   DEVICE=QEMM386.SYS I=*xxxx-yyyy*

- **NOTES**   Although QEMM usually detects usable memory locations automatically, sometimes it does not. For example, earlier versions of QEMM almost never considered the ranges B000-B7FF and F000-F7FF mappable, both of which many machines can use. However, INCLUDE must be used with extreme caution and only with a boot floppy disk readily available, since it is easy to "include" an area of memory that would lock your system.

- **EXAMPLE**   Place the following line in your CONFIG.SYS file to include the areas of memory from F000 hex to F5FF hex and to map areas between 640K and 1024K as RAM. This memory will be controlled by QEMM.

   DEVICE=QEMM386.SYS I=F000-F5FF RAM

   See Also   *QEMM386.SYS EXCLUDE, QEMM386.SYS RAM*

QEMM386.SYS LOCKDMA

- **PURPOSE**   Tells QEMM to disable interrupts during DMA (Direct Memory Access) processing.

- **SYNTAX**

   DEVICE=QEMM386.SYS LD

- **EXAMPLE** Include the following line in your CONFIG.SYS file to halt interrupts during DMA processing:

    DEVICE=QEMM386.SYS LD

See Also *QEMM386.SYS DMA*

QEMM386.SYS MAPS

- **PURPOSE** Lets you specify the number of alternate maps available. Alternate maps are used by operating environments, such as DESQview, to speed up multitasking.

If you do not use the DESQview operating environment, this parameter should be set to 0. Otherwise, you specify a number from 0 to 255, indicating the number of alternate maps you want. Each alternate map uses an additional 4K of memory.

As a rule, you should specify one more alternate map than there are programs concurrently running. The default value used is 8.

- **SYNTAX**

    DEVICE=QEMM386.SYS MA=*xxx*

- **EXAMPLE** Include the following line in your CONFIG.SYS file to set the number of alternate maps to 10; to disable all Compaq features except CER, which relocates the Compaq's video ROM; and to set QEMM's initial mode to AUTO:

    DEVICE=QEMM386.SYS MA=10 NCF CER AU

See Also *QEMM386.SYS AUTO, QEMM386.SYS COMPAQ-EGAROM, QEMM386.SYS NOCOMPAQFEATURES*

QEMM386.SYS MEMORY

- **PURPOSE** Specifies the amount of extended memory that QEMM should use, allocated in kilobytes. If you omit this parameter,

QEMM uses all available extended memory. You can specify any number from 128 to 32,128.

- **SYNTAX**

    DEVICE=QEMM386.SYS ME=*xxxxx*

- **EXAMPLE** Include the following line in your CONFIG.SYS file to specify 800K of extended memory for QEMM and to instruct QEMM to consider the high memory area already allocated and not to look for top memory:

    DEVICE=QEMM386.SYS ME=800 NOHMA NT

See Also *QEMM386.SYS EXTMEM, QEMM386.SYS NOHMA, QEMM386.SYS NOTOPMEMORY*

QEMM386.SYS NOCOMPAQFEATURES

- **PURPOSE** Disables all of the special features provided for Compaq computers with QEMM. During installation, if QEMM detects that it is being run on a Compaq computer it turns on the Compaq-specific features COMPAQEGAROM, COMPAQHALF-ROM, and COMPAQROMMEMORY. You turn these features off with this parameter. You may turn an individual parameter back on by specifying it on the syntax line.

- **SYNTAX**

    DEVICE=QEMM386.SYS NCF

- **EXAMPLE** Include the following line in your CONFIG.SYS file to turn off all Compaq memory management features except COMPAQROMMEMORY:

    DEVICE=QEMM386.SYS NCF CRM

See Also *QEMM386.SYS COMPAQ386S, QEMM386.SYS COMPAQEGAROM, QEMM386.SYS COMPAQHALFROM, QEMM386.SYS COMPAQROMMEMORY*

QEMM386.SYS NOEMS

- **PURPOSE** Tells QEMM not to provide any expanded memory services. Use this parameter only if you have another memory manager that you would rather use to take care of managing expanded memory services.

- **SYNTAX**

  DEVICE=QEMM386.SYS NOEMS

- **EXAMPLE** Include the following line in your CONFIG.SYS file to eliminate QEMM's expanded memory services, to tell QEMM to fill in areas of high memory with no RAM or ROM mapped to them, to put the area of memory between 0C00 hex and 0FFF hex under QEMM's control, and to tell QEMM you're using PC-DOS 4.00 with the /x instruction:

  DEVICE=QEMM386.SYS NOEMS RAM I=0C00-0FFF D4

  See Also   *QEMM386.SYS DOS4, QEMM386.SYS INCLUDE, QEMM386.SYS NOXMS, QEMM386.SYS RAM*

QEMM386.SYS NOFILL

- **PURPOSE** Tells QEMM not to fill conventional memory below 640K. This parameter is useful only if your computer has less than 640K of conventional memory. When you specify it, QEMM does not use any of the memory mapped to the area below 640K. Note that if you specify the NOFILL parameter, you cannot use the NOVIDEOFILL parameter.

- **SYNTAX**

  DEVICE=QEMM386.SYS NO

- **EXAMPLE** Include the following line in your CONFIG.SYS file to prevent filling conventional memory below 640K with extended memory and to disable expanded memory support:

    DEVICE=QEMM386.SYS NO NOEMS

See Also *QEMM386.SYS NOEMS, QEMM386.SYS NOVIDEOFILL*

QEMM386.SYS NOHMA

- **PURPOSE** Tells QEMM to consider the XMS high memory area (HMA) already allocated and not to use it. Use this parameter if there was an XMS driver loaded before QEMM was loaded, and the HMA is already being allocated.

- **SYNTAX**

    DEVICE=QEMM386.SYS NOHMA

- **EXAMPLE** Include the following line in your CONFIG.SYS file to have QEMM consider the HMA high memory area already allocated, to tell QEMM not to sort memory by its speed, to disable all Compaq features, and to set the maximum length of a direct memory access transfer to 85K:

    DEVICE=QEMM386.SYS NOHMA NS NCF DM=85

See Also *QEMM386.SYS DMA, QEMM386.SYS NOCOMPAQ-FEATURES, QEMM386.SYS NOSORT, QEMM386.SYS NOXMS*

QEMM386.SYS NOPAUSEONERROR

- **PURPOSE** Tells QEMM not to pause when it outputs an error or other message to the screen. Under the default PAUSE setting, upon finding an error, QEMM pauses and displays a prompt asking you to press any key to continue or press **Esc** to abort. If you specify this parameter, QEMM will not display this message.

● **SYNTAX**

   DEVICE=QEMM386.SYS NOPE

● **EXAMPLE**   Include the following line in your CONFIG.SYS file to instruct QEMM not to pause:

   DEVICE=QEMM386.SYS NOPE

See Also   *QEMM386.SYS PAUSE*

QEMM386.SYS NOROM

● **PURPOSE**   Instructs QEMM not to map a special reboot page of system ROM into memory. Usually, QEMM tries to map one 4K page of system ROM in order to detect system reboot. If your computer can detect reboot without this, you can save 4K of memory by specifying the NOROM parameter.

● **SYNTAX**

   DEVICE=QEMM386.SYS NR

● **EXAMPLE**   Include the following line in your CONFIG.SYS file to tell QEMM not to map the reboot page of system ROM, not to use shadow RAM, not to sort memory by its speed, and not to look for top memory:

   DEVICE=QEMM386.SYS NR NOSH NS NT

See Also   *QEMM386.SYS NOSHADOWRAM, QEMM386.SYS NOSORT, QEMM386.SYS NOTOPMEMORY*

QEMM386.SYS NOROMHOLES

● **PURPOSE**   Lets you disable QEMM's automatic detection of unused memory addresses in ROM, called ROM holes. Many system

BIOS chips leave large areas of memory unused, which QEMM usually tries to detect automatically. However, this auto-detection scheme sometimes does not work correctly. If some system functions don't work properly when you first install QEMM and continue to give you problems as you are using your computer, try specifying this parameter to see if it corrects the problems.

- SYNTAX

DEVICE=QEMM386.SYS NRH

- **EXAMPLE**   Include the following line in your CONFIG.SYS file to instruct QEMM to disable the automatic detection of ROM holes and not to fill video memory; to set the number of internal data structures for use when multitasking to 25; and to specify that the method for determining the amount of extended memory is non-standard:

DEVICE=QEMM386.SYS NRH NV TA=25 UX

See Also   *QEMM386.SYS NOVIDEOFILL, QEMM386.SYS TASKS, QEMM386.SYS UNUSUALEXT*

QEMM386.SYS NOSHADOWRAM

- **PURPOSE**   Tells QEMM not to use shadow RAM.

- SYNTAX

DEVICE=QEMM386.SYS NOSH

- **NOTES**   Computers with the Chips & Technologies 386 ROM set or the NEAT chip set put 384K of reserved memory in a region in low memory referred to as "shadow RAM." Typically, QEMM determines if your computer has shadow RAM capability and then makes use of it. If QEMM cannot detect it, you need to use this parameter.

- **EXAMPLE** Include the following line in your CONFIG.SYS file to disable the use of shadow RAM; to tell QEMM to pause the display when a message is output to the screen and not to provide expanded memory services; to set the watchdog timer for use on a Compaq Deskpro 386 computer; and to tell QEMM you're using PC-DOS 4.00 with the /X instruction:

    DEVICE=QEMM386.SYS NOSH PAUSE NOEMS WD=2 D4

See Also *QEMM386.SYS DOS4, QEMM386.SYS NOEMS, QEMM-386.SYS PAUSE, QEMM386.SYS WATCHDOG*

QEMM386.SYS NOSORT

- **PURPOSE** Tells QEMM not to sort memory by speed. When QEMM operates, it tests the speed of all available memory and uses the fastest memory first. Use this parameter to tell QEMM to use the memory in the order it finds it, instead of by the memory's relative speed.

- *SYNTAX*

    DEVICE=QEMM386.SYS NS

- **EXAMPLE** Include the following line in your CONFIG.SYS file to tell QEMM to use all memory in the order in which it finds it; to turn QEMM on as a memory manager; and to disable all Compaq features except CER, which relocates Compaq video ROM, and CHR, which turns on Compaq's ability to split system ROM in half:

    DEVICE=QEMM386.SYS NS ON NCF CER CHR

See Also *QEMM386.SYS COMPAQEGAROM, QEMM386.SYS COMPAQHALFROM, QEMM386.SYS NOCOMPAQFEATURES, QEMM386.SYS ON*

QEMM386.SYS NOTOPMEMORY

- **PURPOSE** Instructs QEMM to overlook top memory in your computer and not to use it. Some computers put 384K of memory just below the top of the 16Mb address space. This memory is referred to as "top memory." When QEMM starts it tests to see if there is any top memory available; if there is, QEMM will try to make use of it.

- **SYNTAX**

   DEVICE=QEMM386.SYS NT

- **EXAMPLE** Include the following line in your CONFIG.SYS file to tell QEMM not to look for top memory, to work with a version of DESQview prior to version 2.01, and to turn QEMM on as a memory manager; and to specify that 255K of extended memory should not be used by QEMM:

   DEVICE=QEMM386.SYS NT ODV ON EXT=255

See Also *QEMM386.SYS EXTMEM, QEMM386.SYS OLDDV, QEMM386.SYS ON*

QEMM386.SYS NOVIDEOFILL

- **PURPOSE** Tells QEMM not to fill video memory. On computers with a monochrome or CGA video adapter card, QEMM will usually map the extra memory addresses that are not being used to addresses in high memory. This parameter tells QEMM not to fill this memory, which is located from A000 hex to B7FF hex.

- **SYNTAX**

   DEVICE=QEMM386.SYS NV

- **EXAMPLE**   Include the following line in your CONFIG.SYS file to tell QEMM not to fill video memory, not to move the extended BIOS data area, to eliminate extended memory services, and to fill in areas of high memory that don't have RAM or ROM mapped to them:

    DEVICE=QEMM386.SYS NV NX NOXMS RAM

See Also   *QEMM386.SYS NOFILL, QEMM386.SYS NOXBDA, QEMM386.SYS NOXMS, QEMM386.SYS RAM*

QEMM386.SYS NOVIDEORAM

- **PURPOSE**   Tells QEMM that you do not want to use video RAM as conventional memory.

- **SYNTAX**

    DEVICE=QEMM386.SYS NVR

- **EXAMPLE**   Include the following line in your CONFIG.SYS file to instruct QEMM not to use video RAM as conventional memory and not to sort memory by its speed:

    DEVICE=QEMM386.SYS NVR NS

See Also   *QEMM386.SYS NOSORT, QEMM386.SYS VIDRAMEGA, QEMM386.SYS VIDRAMEMS*

QEMM386.SYS NOWINDOWS3

- **PURPOSE**   Lets you disable the features built into QEMM which support the running of Microsoft Windows 3.0 in Standard mode. Even if you specify this command, you can still run Windows 3.0 in Real mode.

- **SYNTAX**

    DEVICE=QEMM386.SYS NW3

- **NOTES** Using this parameter with QEMM saves about 1K of memory.

- **EXAMPLE** Include the following line in your CONFIG.SYS file to disable support for Windows 3.0 Standard mode:

    DEVICE=QEMM386.SYS NW3

QEMM386.SYS NOXBDA

- **PURPOSE** Tells QEMM that it should not relocate the extended BIOS data area, which is a location of memory mapped at the 639K location. On certain computers, QEMM automatically moves this area to addresses used by QEMM.

- **SYNTAX**

    DEVICE=QEMM386.SYS NX

- **NOTES** A program which incorrectly assumes that the extended BIOS data area is at its original place in memory won't work properly. Use this parameter to disable the remapping of this area so your program will work correctly.

- **EXAMPLE** Include the following line in your CONFIG.SYS file to instruct QEMM not to relocate the extended BIOS data area, to set the size of the DMA buffer to 57K, and to map any memory holes in the range 640K to 1024K as RAM:

    DEVICE=QEMM386.SYS NX DM=57 RAM

    See Also *QEMM386.SYS DMA, QEMM386.SYS RAM*

QEMM386.SYS NOXMS

- **PURPOSE** Instructs QEMM not to act as an extended memory manager, one of the features QEMM normally provides. This parameter

94 QEMM, the Quarterdeck Expanded Memory Manager

will disable the extended memory management feature. Use it only if you must use a separate extended memory manager.

● **SYNTAX**

DEVICE=QEMM386.SYS NOXMS

● **EXAMPLE** Include the following line in your CONFIG.SYS file to disable QEMM as an extended memory manager, to turn QEMM on as a memory manager, to tell QEMM you're using PC-DOS 4.00 with the /X instruction, to set the watchdog timer for use on a PS/2 computer, and to set the size of a SCSI hard drive disk buffer to 128K:

DEVICE=QEMM386.SYS NOXMS ON D4 WD=1 DB=128

See Also *QEMM386.SYS DISKBUF, QEMM386.SYS DOS4, QEMM386.SYS EMBMEM, QEMM386.SYS NOEMS, QEMM386.-SYS NOHMA, QEMM386.SYS ON, QEMM386.SYS WATCHDOG*

QEMM386.SYS OFF

● **PURPOSE** Specifies that expanded memory is not available and turns QEMM off as a memory manager.

● **SYNTAX**

DEVICE=QEMM386.SYS OF

● **EXAMPLE** Include the following line in your CONFIG.SYS file to switch QEMM off:

DEVICE=QEMM386.SYS OF

See Also *QEMM386.SYS AUTO, QEMM386.SYS ON*

QEMM386.SYS OLDDV

- **PURPOSE** Makes QEMM compatible with DESQview versions 1.3 and 2.00. Use it when you're using QEMM 5.1 with an old version of DESQview. This parameter is not necessary if you use DESQview versions 2.01 and above.

- **SYNTAX**

    DEVICE=QEMM386.SYS ODV

- **EXAMPLE** Include the following line in your CONFIG.SYS file to use QEMM 5.1 with version 1.3 of DESQview and with PC-DOS 4.00 with the /X instruction; to set the number of alternate maps to 64; and to disable support for HIMEM.SYS:

    DEVICE=QEMM386.SYS ODV D4 MA=64 IA

See Also *QEMM386.SYS DOS4, QEMM386.SYS IGNOREA20, QEMM386.SYS MAPS*

QEMM386.SYS ON

- **PURPOSE** Tells QEMM that expanded memory is available and that the processor is in virtual 8086 mode. This parameter effectively switches QEMM on.

- **SYNTAX**

    DEVICE=QEMM386.SYS ON

- **EXAMPLE** Include the following line in your CONFIG.SYS file to turn QEMM on:

    DEVICE=QEMM386.SYS ON

See Also *QEMM386.SYS AUTO, QEMM386.SYS OFF*

QEMM386.SYS PAUSE

- **PURPOSE** Tells QEMM to halt the display briefly when it outputs messages to the screen. If a message (usually an error message) occurs while this parameter is in effect, QEMM will prompt you to press any key to continue or press **Esc** to abort. This gives you a chance to read the message before it scrolls off the screen.

- **SYNTAX**

    DEVICE=QEMM386.SYS PAUSE

- **NOTES** PAUSE is the default setting. Turn it off by using the NOPAUSEONERROR parameter.

- **EXAMPLE** Include the following line in your CONFIG.SYS file to tell QEMM to pause the display any time a message is displayed, to disable extended memory services, and to tell QEMM not to sort memory by its speed and not to look for top memory:

    DEVICE=QEMM386.SYS PAUSE NOXMS NS NT

See Also *QEMM386.SYS NOPAUSEONERROR, QEMM386.SYS NOSORT, QEMM386.SYS NOTOPMEMORY, QEMM386.SYS NOXMS*

QEMM386.SYS RAM

- **PURPOSE** Tells QEMM to map areas of memory above 640K and below 1024K that are not being accessed and to use them with the LOADHI program. You can then use this area of memory for other programs.

You can either specify the address range to use or not specify any addresses and let QEMM automatically detect the appropriate memory addresses. If you use this parameter, the initial state of QEMM is forced to ON and cannot be changed.

• SYNTAX

DEVICE=QEMM386.SYS RAM=*xxxx-yyyy*

• **EXAMPLE** Include the following line in your CONFIG.SYS file to tell QEMM to detect unused memory automatically and fill it, not to use shadow RAM, to disable automatic detection of unused addresses in ROM, and that the method for determining the amount of extended memory is nonstandard:

DEVICE=QEMM386.SYS RAM NOSH NRH UX

See Also *QEMM386.SYS NOROMHOLES, QEMM386.SYS NO-SHADOWRAM, QEMM386.SYS ROM, QEMM386.SYS UNUSUALEXT*

QEMM386.SYS ROM

• **PURPOSE** Tells QEMM the areas of ROM that should be copied to RAM and then mapped into their original location in ROM. Since RAM usually operates faster than ROM, copying ROM into RAM and then remapping it will result in faster system operation.

• SYNTAX

DEVICE=QEMM386.SYS ROM=*xxxx-yyyy*

• **NOTES** You can specify the addresses of the range of ROM you want QEMM to map to RAM, or you can specify the beginning address only, and QEMM will automatically detect the length of the ROM area it should relocate. Alternatively, you can use the ROM parameter without specifying any addresses, and QEMM will remap all ROM. Using the ROM parameter forces QEMM into the ON mode, and it cannot be switched off.

• **EXAMPLE** Include the following line in your CONFIG.SYS file to map an EGA ROM into RAM, specifying only the beginning address; to set the maximum length of a direct memory access transfer to 12K; to tell QEMM to consider the HMA high memory already allocated; and not to fill conventional memory below 640K:

DEVICE=QEMM386.SYS ROM=C000 DM=12 NOHMA NO

See Also   *QEMM386.SYS DMA, QEMM386.SYS NOFILL, QEMM-386.SYS NOHMA, QEMM386.SYS RAM*

QEMM386.SYS TASKS

- **PURPOSE**   Lets you specify the number of internal data structures used by QEMM.SYS when QEMM handles interrupts out of protected mode. The default is 16 tasks. Each task requires 384 bytes of extended memory.

- **SYNTAX**

  DEVICE=QEMM386.SYS TA=*xx*

- **EXAMPLE**   Include the following line in your CONFIG.SYS file to set the number of internal data structures to 10; to tell QEMM not to sort memory by its speed and to turn itself on as a memory manager only when a program requires expanded memory; and to set the size of a SCSI hard drive disk buffer to 64K:

  DEVICE=QEMM386.SYS TA=10 NS AU DB=64

See Also   *QEMM386.SYS AUTO, QEMM386.SYS DISKBUF, QEMM386.SYS NOSORT*

QEMM386.SYS UNUSUAL8042

- **PURPOSE**   Tells QEMM that your computer has a nonstandard keyboard controller. The 8042 keyboard controller is used in most IBM-compatible computers. If you start having problems

QEMM386.SYS 99

typing characters from your keyboard after you set QEMM.SYS to ON, it is a good possibility that you have an unusual keyboard controller, and you should use this parameter.

- **SYNTAX**

DEVICE=QEMM386.SYS U8

- **EXAMPLE** Include the following line in your CONFIG.SYS file to tell QEMM that you have an unusual keyboard controller and that it should not monitor the 8042 port; to specify 1024K as the amount of extended memory QEMM should use for itself and for expanded memory; and to tell QEMM not to use shadow RAM:

DEVICE=QEMM386.SYS U8 IA ME=1024 NOSH

See Also *QEMM386.SYS IGNOREA20, QEMM386.SYS MEMORY, QEMM386.SYS NOSHADOWRAM*

QEMM386.SYS UNUSUALEXT

- **PURPOSE** Tells QEMM that the method used to determine the amount of extended memory is a nonstandard method. If your computer does not start correctly with QEMM, using this parameter might fix the problem.

- **SYNTAX**

DEVICE=QEMM386.SYS UX

- **EXAMPLE** Include the following line in your CONFIG.SYS file to tell QEMM that your computer uses a nonstandard method to determine the amount of extended memory available, to tell QEMM not to look for top memory, to set the number of alternate handles at 64, and to tell QEMM you're using a version of DESQview prior to 2.01:

DEVICE=QEMM386.SYS UX NT HA=64 ODV

100 QEMM, the Quarterdeck Expanded Memory Manager

See Also *QEMM386.SYS HANDLES, QEMM386.SYS NOTOPMEMORY, QEMM386.SYS OLDDV*

QEMM386.SYS VIDRAMEGA

- **PURPOSE** Tells QEMM that the video area is not to be mappable.

- **SYNTAX**

   DEVICE=QEMM386.SYS VREGA

- **EXAMPLE** Include the following line in your CONFIG.SYS file to specify that you do not want the video area to be mappable and to set the number of expanded memory handles to 128:

   DEVICE=QEMM386.SYS VREGA HA=128

See Also *QEMM386.SYS HANDLES, QEMM386.SYS NOVIDEORAM, QEMM386.SYS VIDRAMEMS*

QEMM386.SYS VIDRAMEMS

- **PURPOSE** Tells QEMM that the video area is mappable, but it is not a part of conventional memory, nor will it be converted to high memory.

- **SYNTAX**

   DEVICE=QEMM386.SYS VREMS

- **EXAMPLE** Include the following line in your CONFIG.SYS file to tell QEMM that the video area is mappable but is not a part of conventional memory:

   DEVICE=QEMM386.SYS VREMS

See Also *QEMM386.SYS NOVIDEORAM, QEMM386.SYS VIDRAMEGA*

QEMM386.SYS WATCHDOG

- **PURPOSE** Lets you tell QEMM what type of protection level to set. It works in conjunction with the "Protection Level" field found on the DESQview Specify Program Information Advanced Options screen.

- **SYNTAX**

    DEVICE=QEMM386.SYS WD=*x*

- **NOTES** You can set varying levels of protection when running DESQview. Setting the watchdog to 0 in QEMM386.SYS means there should be no watchdog timer. Set it to 1 to use the watchdog feature on a PS/2-compatible computer. Set the watchdog to 2 to use the feature on a Compaq computer.

- **EXAMPLE** Include the following line in your CONFIG.SYS file to tell QEMM to use a Compaq-style watchdog timer; to set the number of internal data structures for use when multitasking to 24; to disable extended memory services; and to tell QEMM to fill in areas of memory that don't have RAM or ROM mapped to them and not to sort memory by its speed:

    DEVICE=QEMM386.SYS WD=2 TA=24 NOXMS RAM NS

See Also *QEMM386.SYS NOSORT, QEMM386.SYS NOXMS, QEMM386.SYS RAM, QEMM386.SYS TASKS, Specify Program Information* (Part II)

QEMM.COM

The QEMM.COM program lets you take control of the Quarterdeck Expanded Memory Manager while you're in DOS. In contrast to QEMM386.SYS, which controls the memory manager from the CONFIG.SYS file with parameters that remain in effect for the entire session, QEMM.COM lets you change parameters as you work.

You can put QEMM.COM in the ON, OFF, or AUTO mode. You can also use QEMM.COM to report status information about the QEMM386.SYS device driver and to check quickly on the status of your system's first megabyte of memory. Most of the information displayed by QEMM.COM is reported by the Manifest memory analysis program in a more complete and user-friendly fashion. (See Part IV of this book.)

To use QEMM.COM, you start at the DOS prompt and type the program's name followed by the name of a parameter. For example, to display a descriptive list of all the parameters available under QEMM.COM, type

QEMM HELP

and press ↵.

QEMM.COM ?

- **PURPOSE**   Lists all the command line parameters available with QEMM.COM. (For a list of the parameters with a description of what they do, see *QEMM.COM HELP*.)

- **SYNTAX**

   QEMM ?

See Also   *QEMM.COM HELP*

QEMM.COM ACCESSED

- **PURPOSE** Displays a list of memory regions, measured in multiples of 4K, indicating whether and how they have been accessed by other programs running on your system.

- **SYNTAX**

   QEMM ACCESSED

- **NOTES** This parameter will give you a good idea of which areas of memory in your computer have and which have not been used. You can use it to determine the size of a program and whether the program accesses or writes to a certain area of high memory.

ACCESSED reports the size of all programs you've run since QEMM was turned on in the current session. To ascertain the size of a specific program, type **QEMM RESET** at the DOS prompt to reset all memory areas to "unaccessed." Then run the program you want to learn about, use some of its features, and exit. Return to the DOS prompt, and type **QEMM ACCESSED**.

The display, illustrated in Figure III.1, lists memory locations by address and indicates whether they have been accessed, unaccessed,

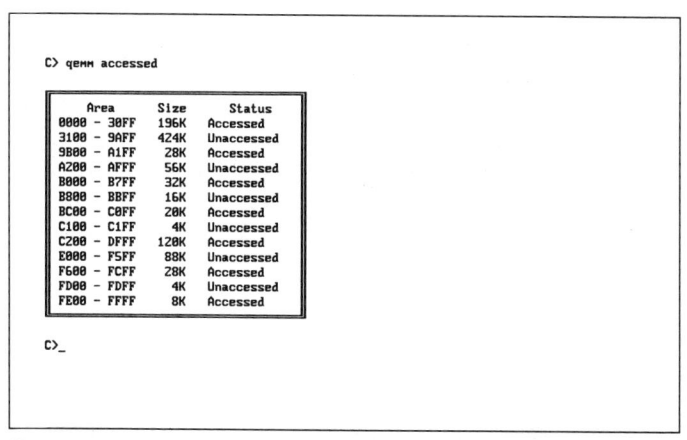

```
C> qemm accessed

    Area       Size    Status
  0000 - 30FF   196K   Accessed
  3100 - 9AFF   424K   Unaccessed
  9B00 - A1FF    28K   Accessed
  A200 - AFFF    56K   Unaccessed
  B000 - B7FF    32K   Accessed
  B800 - BBFF    16K   Unaccessed
  BC00 - C0FF    20K   Accessed
  C100 - C1FF     4K   Unaccessed
  C200 - DFFF   120K   Accessed
  E000 - F5FF    88K   Unaccessed
  F600 - FCFF    28K   Accessed
  FD00 - FDFF     4K   Unaccessed
  FE00 - FFFF     8K   Accessed

C>_
```

Figure III.1: The QEMM ACCESSED parameter screen

or written to. *Accessed* locations have been read by a program. *Unaccessed* areas have been neither read nor written to. *Written to* locations contain stored data but no program code.

See Also *QEMM.COM ACCESSED MAP, QEMM.COM RESET*

QEMM.COM ACCESSED MAP

• **PURPOSE** Displays a map of the memory areas, measured in multiples of 4K, which have been accessed by other programs running on your system.

• **SYNTAX**

QEMM ACCESSED MAP

• **NOTES** The ACCESSED MAP parameter gives you the same information as the ACCESSED parameter, but in map rather than list format (see Figure III.2). See the entry for QEMM.COM ACCESSED for detailed information about how to use this parameter.

See Also *QEMM.COM ACCESSED, QEMM.COM RESET*

```
C>qemm accessed map

    n=0123 4567 89AB CDEF
 0n00 UUUU AAAA AUUU UUUU
 1n00 UUUU UUUU UUUU UUUU
 2n00 UUUU UUUU UUUU UUUU
 3n00 UUUU UUUU UUUU UUUU
 4n00 UUUU UUUU UUUU UUUU
 5n00 UUUU UUUU UUUU UUUU
 6n00 UUUU UUUU UUUU UUUU     U = Unaccessed
 7n00 UUUU UUUU UUUU UUUU     A = Accessed
 8n00 UUUU UUUU UUUU UUUU     W = Written
 9n00 UUUU UUUU UUUU UUUU
 An00 UUUU UUUU UUUU UUUU
 Bn00 UUUU UUUU UUUU UUUU
 Cn00 AUAA AAAA UUUU UUUU
 Dn00 UUUU UUUU UUUU UUUU
 En00 UUUU UUUU UUUU UUUU
 Fn00 UUUU UUWA AAAW AUAA

C>_
```

Figure III.2: The QEMM ACCESSED MAP parameter screen.

QEMM.COM ANALYSIS

- **PURPOSE** Provides information about the use of conventional memory in your system that allows you to configure QEMM386.SYS to make the best use of that memory. ANALYSIS displays a list of memory regions by address, showing which regions are being used to their full potential and which regions should be either "Excluded" or "Included" by designating the appropriate QEMM386.SYS parameter in your CONFIG.SYS file.

- **SYNTAX**

    QEMM ANALYSIS

- **NOTES** In order for the ANALYSIS procedure to make an accurate assessment of the memory used by your programs, you must first run all the programs you usually use, making sure you perform all their functions. If you have DESQview, load it but quit immediately without running any programs.

You should also access all the hardware on your system. Format a diskette on each of your floppy disk drives. Run a communications program to access the serial ports. Use all the monitors you have. Print a document to make use of your printer. Load your network drivers and log on to your network.

However, do not run any utilities that check the functioning of your computer, and especially do not run a memory test program. Failing to follow all the prescribed procedures will cause ANALYSIS to give inaccurate results.

After you have made use of every function on your computer, type the parameter syntax at the DOS prompt. The display will report either "OK," "Exclude," or "Include" for each memory address.

OK means that ANALYSIS was run correctly and QEMM is working appropriately with those memory areas.

Exclude indicates areas of memory with which QEMM is not working properly. You should use the EXCLUDE parameter on the QEMM386.SYS line in your CONFIG.SYS file to prevent QEMM from using these areas.

Include specifies areas of memory that have not been used by a program but which have been reserved by QEMM for internal housekeeping. You should use the INCLUDE parameter on the QEMM386.SYS line in your CONFIG.SYS file to allow QEMM to use these areas for programs.

See Also   *QEMM.COM ANALYSIS MAP, QEMM386.SYS EXCLUDE, QEMM386.SYS INCLUDE*

QEMM.COM ANALYSIS MAP

- **PURPOSE**   Provides information about the use of conventional memory in your system.

- **SYNTAX**

   QEMM ANALYSIS MAP

- **NOTES**   ANALYSIS MAP provides the same information, displayed in map format, as the ANALYSIS parameter gives in list format. See the entry for QEMM.COM ANALYSIS for detailed information about how to use this parameter.

See Also   *QEMM.COM ANALYSIS*

QEMM.COM AUTO

- **PURPOSE**   Tells QEMM to turn itself on only when a program needs expanded memory. If not specified otherwise, QEMM starts out in the AUTO mode.

- **SYNTAX**

   QEMM AUTO

See Also   *QEMM.COM OFF, QEMM.COM ON*

QEMM.COM HELP

- **PURPOSE** Displays a list of all QEMM.COM parameters with a description of what each one does.

- **SYNTAX**

    QEMM HELP

See Also   *QEMM.COM ?*

QEMM.COM MAP

- **PURPOSE** Instructs QEMM.COM to display reports in a map format when combined with the ACCESSED, ANALYSIS, or TYPE parameters.

- **SYNTAX**

    QEMM *parameter* **MAP**

- **NOTES** Usually, QEMM displays its reports in a list format. By using the MAP parameter as a modifier, you will be able to see the reports in a graphic rather than text format.

See Also   *QEMM.COM ACCESSED, QEMM.COM ANALYSIS, QEMM.COM TYPE*

QEMM.COM MEMORY

- **PURPOSE** Reports how your computer's memory is used both before and after QEMM has configured it.

- **SYNTAX**

    QEMM MEMORY

108 QEMM, the Quarterdeck Expanded Memory Manager

- **NOTES** This parameter reports in detail on conventional memory, high memory, extended memory, and expanded memory. Certain computers will display additional information. For example, if you are using a Compaq computer, you may see an entry called "Top Memory." If you are using a machine based on the Chips & Technologies chip sets, you will see an entry for "Shadow RAM."

Four columns in the MEMORY screen display, illustrated in Figure III.3, describe the memory in your computer. *Initial* shows the amount of memory available before QEMM configured it. *Unavailable to QEMM* indicates memory taken up by software and by hardware drivers which were loaded before QEMM was. The *Converted by QEMM* column shows what QEMM does to your memory. The *Leaving* column tells you how much memory is left over once QEMM is finished initializing itself.

QEMM.COM NOPAUSEONERROR

- **PURPOSE** Tells QEMM.COM not to pause when it finds an error. Usually, upon finding an error, QEMM displays a message telling you to press any key to continue or press **Esc** to abort. Specifying this parameter instructs QEMM not to pause and display this message.

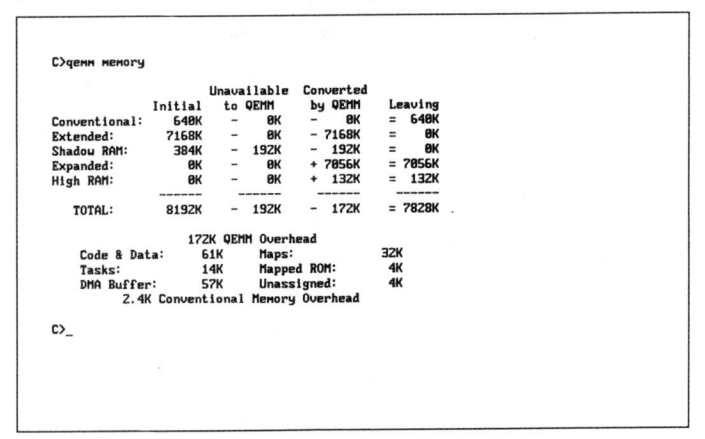

```
C>qemm memory

                    Unavailable  Converted
            Initial   to QEMM    by QEMM    Leaving
Conventional:  640K  -    0K   -     0K   =   640K
Extended:     7168K  -    0K   -  7168K   =     0K
Shadow RAM:    384K  -  192K   -   192K   =     0K
Expanded:        0K  -    0K   +  7056K   =  7056K
High RAM:        0K  -    0K   +   132K   =   132K
              ------   ------    ------     ------
   TOTAL:     8192K  -  192K   -   172K   =  7828K

              172K QEMM Overhead
   Code & Data:   61K   Maps:           32K
   Tasks:         14K   Mapped ROM:      4K
   DMA Buffer:    57K   Unassigned:      4K
        2.4K Conventional Memory Overhead

C>_
```

Figure III.3: The QEMM MEMORY parameter screen

- **SYNTAX**

    QEMM NOPE

See Also *QEMM.COM PAUSE*

QEMM.COM OFF

- **PURPOSE** Specifies that expanded memory is not available and turns QEMM off as a memory manager.

- **SYNTAX**

    QEMM OFF

See Also *QEMM.COM AUTO, QEMM.COM ON*

QEMM.COM ON

- **PURPOSE** Tells QEMM that expanded memory is available and that the processor is in virtual 8086 mode. This parameter effectively turns QEMM on.

- **SYNTAX**

    QEMM ON

See Also *QEMM.COM AUTO, QEMM.COM OFF*

QEMM.COM PAUSE

- **PURPOSE** Tells QEMM to halt the display briefly when it outputs messages to the screen. Use this parameter to tell QEMM always to stop and prompt you to press a key to continue when a message is displayed. This prevents valuable information from being scrolled off the screen before you have a chance to read it.

- **SYNTAX**

    QEMM PAUSE

    See Also *QEMM.COM NOPAUSEONERROR*

QEMM.COM RESET

- **PURPOSE** Resets the state of all memory areas to Unaccessed. This is useful because when you're using the ACCESSED parameter, it is sometimes handy to reset all memory to Unaccessed to ascertain the areas of memory which are being accessed by a specific program. See the entry for QEMM.COM ACCESSED for more information.

- **SYNTAX**

    QEMM RESET

    See Also *QEMM.COM ACCESSED*

QEMM.COM SUMMARY

- **PURPOSE** Presents a brief listing of valuable status information about how QEMM is working. With this parameter, you can find out what mode the memory manager is in, how much expanded memory is available, and the address of the page frame used for expanded memory services.

- **SYNTAX**

    QEMM SUMMARY

QEMM.COM TYPE

- **PURPOSE** Presents a list showing how the first megabyte of memory is being used by QEMM. Use this report to determine the effect of QEMM memory management on your system.

QEMM.COM   111

- **SYNTAX**

    QEMM TYPE

- **NOTES**   Several terms are used in the TYPE screen display to describe your memory. *Mappable* areas of memory can be mapped into, using EMS specifications. *Rammable* refers to memory areas which can be mapped into by QEMM but which are too small to be accessed by EMS specifications. A *Page Frame* is an area of memory measuring 64K that is used to access EMS expanded memory.

High RAM describes areas of conventional memory between 640K and 1024K which have been filled with RAM by QEMM. *Mapped ROM* refers to addresses of read-only memory which have been copied to RAM and then remapped into their original addresses by QEMM386.SYS's ROM parameter. *Excluded* refers to areas of memory which have been made unmappable by the EXCLUDE parameter of QEMM386.SYS.

Video refers to memory addresses reserved for use by the video display adapter. *Adapter RAM* regions of memory have had RAM mapped into them by other adapter cards. *ROM* refers to regions of read-only memory which have not been remapped by the QEMM386.SYS ROM parameter. *Split ROM* refers to addresses which QEMM386.SYS has detected as having ROM that occupies only a portion of the 4K area.

See Also   *QEMM.COM EXCLUDE, QEMM.COM ROM, QEMM.-COM TYPE MAP*

QEMM.COM TYPE MAP

- **PURPOSE**   Presents a map showing how the first megabyte of memory in your computer is used.

- **SYNTAX**

    QEMM TYPE MAP

- **NOTES** The output from this command, illustrated in Figure III.4, gives you the same information as that given for the TYPE command, except that it is given in map format. It is sometimes useful to see the information in a map rather than a list format.

See Also   QEMM.COM TYPE

```
>qemm type map

    n=0123 4567 89AB CDEF
0n00 XXXX XXXX XXXX ++++
1n00 ++++ ++++ ++++ ++++
2n00 ++++ ++++ ++++ ++++      + = Mappable
3n00 ++++ ++++ ++++ ++++      x = Rammable
4n00 ++++ ++++ ++++ ++++      F = Page Frame
5n00 ++++ ++++ ++++ ++++      H = High RAM
6n00 ++++ ++++ ++++ ++++      M = Mapped ROM
7n00 ++++ ++++ ++++ ++++      X = Excluded
8n00 ++++ ++++ ++++ ++++      U = Video
9n00 ++++ ++++ ++++ ++++      A = Adapter RAM
An00 UUUU UUUU UUUU UUUU      R = ROM
Bn00 HHHH HHHH UUUU UUUU      / = Split ROM
Cn00 RRRR RRRR HHHH HHHH
Dn00 HHHH HHHH HHHH HHHH
En00 FFFF FFFF FFFF FFFF
Fn00 RRRR RRHR MRRR RRRR

C>_
```

Figure III.4: The QEMM TYPE MAP parameter screen

LOADHI

The LOADHI program lets you free areas of conventional memory by loading programs into high RAM. This is desirable because most programs run in the memory area below 640K, and the more memory available for their use, the better.

Two versions, LOADHI.SYS and LOADHI.COM, allow you to load device drivers, TSRs, and DOS resources into areas of high RAM. Both versions of the program use the same set of parameters.

To load programs into high memory using LOADHI.SYS, type **DEVICE=LOADHI.SYS** in your CONFIG.SYS file, followed by the appropriate LOADHI parameter name. To specify any parameter for more than one program you're running under DESQview, place multiple LOADHI.SYS lines in your CONFIG.SYS file, each line naming a different program.

To load programs using LOADHI.COM, type **LOADHI** at the command line in DOS or type **LOADHI.COM** in your AUTOEXEC.BAT file, followed, in either case, by the appropriate LOADHI parameter name.

If you type **LOADHI** without any parameters at the command line, you will see a report about how the HMA high memory area of your computer is being used.

LOADHI ?

• **PURPOSE** Lists all the command line parameters available for use with the LOADHI program. For a list of the parameters along with a short description of what they do, see *LOADHI HELP*.

• **SYNTAX**

LOADHI ?

See Also *LOADHI HELP*

LOADHI BESTFIT

• **PURPOSE** Instructs LOADHI to use the smallest block of memory your program will fit into when putting it in high memory. Using this parameter usually tends to reserve regions of high memory in proportion to the size of programs.

• **SYNTAX**

LOADHI /B *program*

See Also *LOADHI GETSIZE, LOADHI SIZE*

LOADHI EXCLUDELARGEST

- **PURPOSE** Instructs LOADHI not to use the largest region of memory to load your target program. Specifying a value (*n*) for this parameter tells LOADHI not to use the *n*th largest region. If you don't specify a value, LOADHI will find the largest area of memory and refrain from using it.

- **SYNTAX**

    LOADHI /XL :*n program*

See Also *LOADHI EXCLUDEREGION, LOADHI EXCLUDESMALLEST*

LOADHI EXCLUDEREGION

- **PURPOSE** Instructs LOADHI not to use the region of memory you specify as *n* on the command line when it is loading a program.

- **SYNTAX**

    LOADHI /XR:*n program*

See Also *LOADHI EXCLUDELARGEST, LOADHI EXCLUDESMALLEST*

LOADHI EXCLUDESMALLEST

- **PURPOSE** Instructs LOADHI not to use the smallest region of memory when it loads your program. Specifying a value (*n*) for this parameter tells LOADHI not to use the *n*th smallest region of memory. If you don't to specify a value, LOADHI will find the smallest area of memory and refrain from using it.

- **SYNTAX**

    LOADHI /XS:*n program*

    See Also *LOADHI EXCLUDELARGEST, LOADHI EXCLUDEREGION*

LOADHI GETSIZE

- **PURPOSE** Reports the exact amount of memory a program requires when it is running. If you specify a *filename*, LOADHI will write the program name and the amount of memory it uses to an external file.

- **SYNTAX**

    LOADHI /GS:*filename program*

    See Also *LOADHI SIZE*

LOADHI HAPPIEST

- **PURPOSE** Tells LOADHI to use the smallest block of memory in which a program will fit, as long as the program will not terminate because of an error. LOADHI will start by loading a program into a certain area of memory. If it does not fit, QEMM finds a larger area of memory and tries loading the program again. QEMM continues this procedure until it can load the program into a memory area large enough to hold the program.

- **SYNTAX**

    LOADHI /H

    See Also *LOADHI EXCLUDELARGEST, LOADHI EXCLUDEREGION, LOADHI EXCLUDESMALLEST*

LOADHI HELP

- **PURPOSE** Displays a list of all LOADHI parameters with a description of what each one does.

- **SYNTAX**

    LOADHI /HELP

See Also *LOADHI ?*

LOADHI LARGEST

- **PURPOSE** Tells LOADHI to load a program into the largest region of memory available. If you specify a value (n), LOADHI will load the program into the nth largest region available.

- **SYNTAX**

    LOADHI /L:*n program*

See Also *LOADHI SMALLEST*

LOADHI LO

- **PURPOSE** Tells LOADHI always to use the lower 640K of conventional memory instead of high RAM when setting aside memory for programs.

- **SYNTAX**

    LOADHI /LO

- **NOTES** This parameter is usually used temporarily to test different LOADHI statements by placing it at the end of a parameter line in your configuration file or a batch file in order to see the results that a parameter or group of parameters might have.

See Also *LOADHI NOLO*

LOADHI NOLO

- **PURPOSE** Tells LOADHI not to load the program specified if it will not fit in high RAM.

- **SYNTAX**

   LOADHI /NL *program*

- **NOTES** Use this parameter to specify that you want to use additional device drivers or DOS resources only if they will fit in high memory.

See Also *LOADHI LO*

LOADHI NOPAUSEONERROR

- **PURPOSE** Tells LOADHI not to pause when it finds an error. Usually, upon finding an error in parameter syntax, LOADHI displays a message telling you to press any key to continue or press **Esc** to abort. If you specify this parameter, LOADHI will not pause and display this message when an error does occur.

- **SYNTAX**

   LOADHI /NOPE

See Also *LOADHI PAUSE*

LOADHI PAUSE

- **PURPOSE** Tells LOADHI to halt the display briefly when it outputs messages to the screen. This prevents valuable information from being scrolled off the screen before you have a chance to read it. Set this parameter to tell LOADHI always to stop and prompt you to press a key to continue when a message is displayed.

- **SYNTAX**

    LOADHI /PAUSE

See Also   *LOADHI NOPAUSEONERROR*

LOADHI REGION

- **PURPOSE**   Tells LOADHI to load the program into a certain numbered memory region, specified as *n*. The value *n* is required with this parameter.

- **SYNTAX**

    LOADHI /R:*n program*

See Also   *LOADHI EXCLUDELARGEST, LOADHI EXCLUDEREGION, LOADHI EXCLUDESMALLEST*

LOADHI SIZE

- **PURPOSE**   Instructs LOADHI to allocate memory for a program from a block that will best fit a value you define. Specify the size of the block in bytes, using the syntax shown in the first line below, or in kilobytes, as shown in the second line. To determine what value to specify, use the LOADHI GETSIZE parameter.

- **SYNTAX**

    LOADHI /SIZE:*nnnn program*
    LOADHI /SIZE:*nnnn***K** *program*

See Also   *LOADHI GETSIZE*

LOADHI SMALLEST

- **PURPOSE** Tells LOADHI to load a program into the smallest memory region available. If you specify a value (*n*), LOADHI will use the *n*th smallest region available.

- **SYNTAX**

    LOADHI /S:*n program*

    See Also *LOADHI LARGEST*

LOADHI TERMINATERESIDENT

- **PURPOSE** Tells LOADHI to terminate and stay resident. This parameter suppresses an error message issued by DOS 4 indicating a failure to load a TSR when, in fact, one is loaded. This parameter is useful only if you are using LOADHI in combination with DOS 4's INSTALL command, found in your CONFIG.SYS file.

- **SYNTAX**

    LOADHI /TSR *program*

THE DOS RESOURCE PROGRAMS

The DOS Resource programs are four programs which let you manage the data used by DOS. You may use these programs by themselves or with the LOADHI program.

The Resources that you have control over are BUFFERS, FCBS, FILES, and LASTDRIVE. If you have worked with the CONFIG.SYS file, you are probably familiar with what these resources are for. If you are not familiar with them, see your DOS manual, or see *Mastering DOS* from SYBEX, for detailed information about them.

If you are using DESQview, the DOS Resource programs can be used only to report settings, not to change settings from within DESQview. If you need to change some of the settings, close all your DESQview windows and exit DESQview.

BUFFERS.COM

- **PURPOSE**   Lets you specify the number of buffers DOS should use when loading sectors from disks. A larger number of buffers can usually improve disk drive response time.

- **SYNTAX**

    BUFFERS=*xx*

- **NOTES**   You can set the number of buffers from DOS or from within a batch file. If you don't specify any parameters on the command line, the program will respond by reporting the number of buffers currently available.

To minimize your memory usage, you should set the number of buffers in your CONFIG.SYS file to 1, then use the BUFFERS program in conjunction with LOADHI to create the rest of the buffers for your system.

- **EXAMPLES**   Include the following line in your CONFIG.SYS file to specify a single buffer:

    BUFFERS=1

Include the following line in your AUTOEXEC.BAT file to use expanded memory to set the number of buffers to 35. It is best to use this as the first line in your AUTOEXEC.BAT file, so that the machine will immediately take advantage of the extra buffers.

LOADHI BUFFERS=35

See Also   *FCBS.COM, FILES.COM, LASTDRIVE.COM, LOADHI*

FCBS.COM

- **PURPOSE** Keeps track of the File Control Blocks (FCBS), which oversee the creation of disk files. In versions of DOS since 2.0, the preferred method of file access is the use of file handles. However, the use of file control blocks is still supported in the latest version of DOS for compatibility with older versions.

- **SYNTAX**

    FCBS=*a,b*

- **NOTES** The first number (*a*) you specify in the syntax line tells DOS how many file control blocks to allocate memory for. The second number (*b*) indicates how many of those file control blocks should be protected when DOS needs to close an open file control block.

You can set the number of file control blocks from DOS or in a batch file. If you don't specify any parameters on the command line, the program will respond by reporting the number of file control blocks currently available.

To maximize your memory usage, if you have a line in your CONFIG.SYS file that sets the number of file control blocks, you should remove it. Instead, use the FCBS program in conjunction with LOADHI from the DOS command line or in a batch file to set the desired number and to keep file control blocks out of the first 640K of conventional memory.

- **EXAMPLE** Include the following line in your AUTOEXEC.BAT file to set the number of file control blocks to 8 and to protect 2 of them. High memory will be used to store them.

    LOADHI FCBS=8,2

See Also *BUFFERS.COM, FILES.COM, LASTDRIVE.COM, LOADHI*

FILES.COM

● **PURPOSE** Used to set up or change the number of areas of memory that DOS uses to keep track of disk files.

● **SYNTAX**

FILES=*xx*

● **NOTES** You can set the number of file areas from DOS or in a batch file. If you don't specify any parameters on the command line, the program will respond by reporting the number of file areas currently available.

To maximize your memory usage and avoid potential problems with some programs that have files loaded in high memory, you should set the number of file areas in your CONFIG.SYS file to 20. Then use the FILES program in conjunction with LOADHI to create any additional file areas for your system.

● **EXAMPLES** Include the following line in your CONFIG.SYS file to set the number of FILES to 20:

FILES=20

Include the following line in your AUTOEXEC.BAT file to set your FILES resource to a total of 35. High memory is used for the additional 15 files.

LOADHI FILES=35

See Also *BUFFERS.COM, FCBS.COM, LASTDRIVE.COM, LOADHI*

LASTDRIVE.COM

● **PURPOSE** Lets you specify any drive label from A: to Z: to access both physical and logical disk drives.

- **SYNTAX**

    LASTDRIVE=x

- **NOTES** Use the LASTDRIVE program without any parameters to receive a report identifying your last drive. This DOS Resource is especially useful if you have a subdirectory with a long path name: you can designate the entire path name with a single directory label and access it by typing just a few keystrokes. It is best to use LASTDRIVE in combination with the LOADHI program to store the last drive's data in high memory.

    You should set the LASTDRIVE parameter in your CONFIG.SYS file to the drive letter of your last hard disk partition. Then, use LASTDRIVE in conjunction with LOADHI to reset the last drive and to use high memory to keep track of the new drive letter.

- **EXAMPLES** Include the following line in your CONFIG.SYS file to set the last drive to D: in order to access the subdirectory C:\GRAPHICS\CAD\AUTOCAD\DATA with a single drive designation:

    LASTDRIVE=D

    Include the following line in your AUTOEXEC.BAT file to reset the number of drives to G:, while at the same time using high memory to keep track of the new drive letter:

    LOADHI LASTDRIVE=G

    See Also   *BUFFERS.COM, FCBS.COM, FILES.COM, LOADHI*

THE VIDRAM PROGRAM

VIDRAM is an interesting utility, which will take the memory used by your EGA or VGA video adapter board and convert it for use as conventional memory. VIDRAM increases the amount of conventional memory available on EGA monochrome systems by 64K and on color systems by 96K.

There is a catch, however. When you make use of this extra memory, you cannot use any programs that display graphics. If you never use any graphics programs, you will have no problem using VIDRAM. If you only occasionally use graphics programs, you may still gain the advantages of extra memory by turning VIDRAM on and off.

In order to use VIDRAM, you must first load it from the DOS command line. You can make the best use of it, however, by specifying it in your AUTOEXEC.BAT file, which will load it in the ON mode whenever you turn on your computer. You can then turn it off by specifying the OFF parameter just before you use graphics and turn it back on when you are done with graphics programs, regaining the use of the additional memory.

VIDRAM ?

- **PURPOSE**   Lists all the command line parameters available for use with the VIDRAM program. For a list of the parameters along with a short description of what they do, see *VIDRAM HELP*.

- **SYNTAX**

    VIDRAM ?

See Also   *VIDRAM HELP*

VIDRAM HELP

- **PURPOSE**   Displays a list of all VIDRAM parameters with a description of what each one does.

- **SYNTAX**

    VIDRAM HELP

See Also *VIDRAM ?*

VIDRAM NOCGA

● **PURPOSE** Prevents any graphics functions from being processed by VIDRAM.

● **SYNTAX**

   VIDRAM NOCGA

● **EXAMPLE** Type the following line at the DOS prompt to inform VIDRAM to be present in memory but to prevent any graphics function from being processed:

   VIDRAM NOCGA

See Also *VIDRAM NOEGA*

VIDRAM NOEGA

● **PURPOSE** Prevents EGA- or VGA-requested functions from being processed, while honoring low-resolution CGA-requested functions.

● **SYNTAX**

   VIDRAM NOEGA

● **EXAMPLE** Type the following line at the DOS prompt to let only CGA graphics be processed by VIDRAM:

   VIDRAM NOEGA

See Also *VIDRAM NOCGA*

VIDRAM NOPAUSEONERROR

- **PURPOSE** Tells VIDRAM not to pause when it finds an error. Usually, upon finding a parameter error, VIDRAM displays a message telling you to press any key to continue or **Esc** to abort. Specify this parameter and VIDRAM will not pause to display error messages.

- **SYNTAX**

    VIDRAM NOPE

    See Also *VIDRAM PAUSE*

VIDRAM OFF

- **PURPOSE** Enables you to use graphics programs and prevents the extra video memory from being used as conventional memory. When VIDRAM is first loaded, it is usually in the ON mode. Specify the OFF parameter to run any graphics program.

- **SYNTAX**

    VIDRAM OFF

    See Also *VIDRAM ON*

VIDRAM ON

- **PURPOSE** Loads VIDRAM and makes available an additional 64K of memory on monochrome systems and 96K on color systems, mapped in the first 640K of conventional memory.

- **SYNTAX**

    VIDRAM ON

The VIDRAM Program 127

- **EXAMPLE** Type the following line at the DOS prompt to turn VIDRAM on and create an additional 96K of memory:

    VIDRAM ON

    See Also *VIDRAM OFF*

VIDRAM PAUSE

- **PURPOSE** Tells VIDRAM to halt the display briefly when it outputs messages to the screen. This prevents valuable information from being scrolled off the screen before you have a chance to read it. Set this parameter to tell VIDRAM always to stop and prompt you to press a key to continue when a message is displayed.

- **SYNTAX**

    VIDRAM PAUSE

    See Also *VIDRAM NOPAUSEONERROR*

VIDRAM RESIDENT

- **PURPOSE** Tells VIDRAM to load (or become resident) but not to activate. This way, VIDRAM will be available quickly in case you need to use it.

- **SYNTAX**

    VIDRAM RESIDENT

- **EXAMPLE** Type the following line at the DOS prompt to tell VIDRAM to become resident:

    VIDRAM RESIDENT

VIDRAM VIDRAMEGA

• **PURPOSE**   Tells VIDRAM that the video area is not to be mappable.

• **SYNTAX**

   VIDRAM VIDRAMEGA

• **EXAMPLE**   Type the following line at the DOS prompt to prevent VIDRAM from mapping the video area:

   VIDRAM VIDRAMEGA

See Also   *VIDRAM VIDRAMEMS*

VIDRAM VIDRAMEMS

• **PURPOSE**   Tells VIDRAM that the video area is mappable but is not part of conventional memory, so it should not be converted to high memory. This parameter cannot be used with versions of DESQview previous to 2.26.

• **SYNTAX**

   VIDRAM VIDRAMEMS

• **EXAMPLE**   Type the following line at the DOS prompt to tell VIDRAM that the video area is mappable:

   VIDRAM VIDRAMEMS

EMS2EXT.SYS

Certain programs that require extended memory will not accept EMS memory remapped to extended memory by QEMM. IBM's DisplayWrite and VDISK.SYS, which comes with DOS, are two such programs. You can convert EMS 4.0 expanded memory to extended memory by placing the EMS2EXT.SYS device driver in your CONFIG.SYS file.

• SYNTAX

DEVICE=EMS2EXT.SYS MEMORY=*nnnn* **SPEED**

• **NOTES** Only two parameters need to be used with this program. *Memory* describes the number of kilobytes of expanded memory to allocate for use as extended memory.

Speed is optional and can be set to either FAST memory or SLOW memory.

• **EXAMPLE** Include the following line in your CONFIG.SYS file to tell EMS2EXT to convert 1024K of expanded memory to extended memory. Let the program determine the speed of the memory.

DEVICE=EMS2EXT.SYS MEMORY=1024

Part IV

Manifest Memory Analyzer

Manifest is a system analysis utility from Quarterdeck Office Systems, available separately or bundled with DESQview 386. It provides valuable information about how your system's memory, hardware, and software are set up and configured. If you're an experienced user, you'll find this information extremely helpful; if you're inexperienced, you may need to learn more about your system in order to make full use of Manifest's reports.

132 Manifest Memory Analyzer

Start Manifest by typing **MFT** from the DOS command line or by selecting Quarterdeck **M**anifest from the list of programs on DESQview's Open Window menu. Manifest will immediately display the System Overview report about your computer's memory and hardware.

The Manifest display consists of three sections. The vertical menu panel on the left side of the screen lists up to seven variable categories, which describe various aspects of your system, as well as Hints and Exit.

Major reporting categories include system information, the first megabyte of memory, expanded memory, extended memory, DOS, QEMM-386, and information about DESQview. The category list varies depending upon the hardware and software in your computer. When you select a category, its name is marked with arrows.

Across the top of the screen, a horizontal menu displays a list of topics in the selected category. The topics vary with each category, and the one you select is shown in reverse video.

The center of the screen displays Manifest's analysis of the category and topic you have selected. Figure IV.1 shows the screen display for the Overview topic in the System category.

You may select a category or a topic in any of the three ways you ordinarily make menu selections in DESQview: type the highlighted letter associated with the category or topic name; use the arrow keys to highlight your selection (↑ and ↓ for the vertical category menu, ← and → for the horizontal topic menu), and press ↵ or the **spacebar**; or position the mouse cursor over your selection and click the left mouse button.

To view the Help screen for online assistance regarding a topic, press the **F1** key. To print any screen that is displayed, press the **F2** key and follow the on-screen directions.

Press the **spacebar** to display updated information found on certain screens whose information may change automatically in conjunction with other changes on your system. Terminate Manifest by pressing the **Esc** key twice in succession.

DESQview Memory Status   133

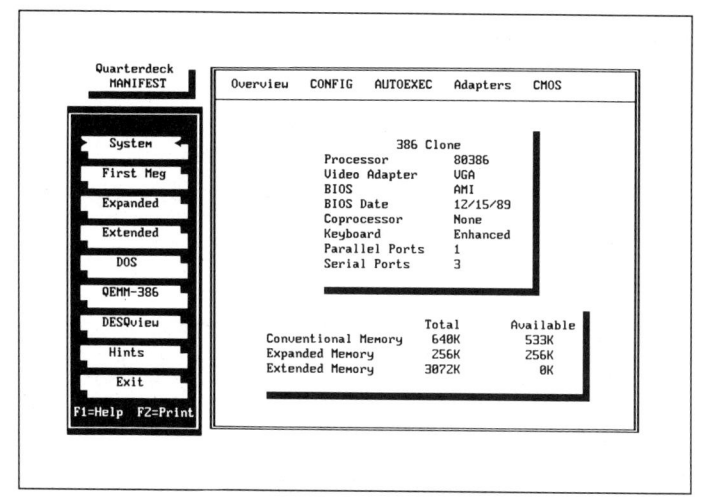

```
    Quarterdeck
    MANIFEST      Overview  CONFIG  AUTOEXEC  Adapters  CMOS

  ┌─────────┐                386 Clone
  │ System  │◄    Processor             80386
  ├─────────┤     Video Adapter         VGA
  │First Meg│     BIOS                  AMI
  ├─────────┤     BIOS Date             12/15/89
  │Expanded │     Coprocessor           None
  ├─────────┤     Keyboard              Enhanced
  │Extended │     Parallel Ports        1
  ├─────────┤     Serial Ports          3
  │  DOS    │
  ├─────────┤
  │QEMM-386 │
  ├─────────┤                     Total       Available
  │DESQview │    Conventional Memory    640K        533K
  ├─────────┤    Expanded Memory        256K        256K
  │  Hints  │    Extended Memory       3072K          0K
  ├─────────┤
  │  Exit   │
  └─────────┘
  F1=Help F2=Print
```

Figure IV.1: The Manifest System Overview screen

The entries that follow are organized alphabetically by category and, within category, by topic. Each entry's heading consists of the category name followed by the topic name. The entries presented here cover the options you'll see displayed if you're using Manifest in DESQview with QEMM-386.

DESQVIEW MEMORY STATUS

- **PURPOSE** Shows information about the amount of memory that is available to DESQview. This screen is similar to the one displayed by DESQview's Memory Status command and appears only if you are running Manifest with DESQview. It lists the common memory, conventional memory, and expanded memory available in your system.

To Display the DESQview Memory Status Screen

1. Select the DESQview category.
2. Select the Memory Status topic.

See Also *DESQview Overview*

DESQVIEW OVERVIEW

● **PURPOSE** Displays information about DESQview and the window in which you are running Manifest. This screen appears only if you are running Manifest with DESQview. When you select this option, you will see a screen that looks like Figure IV.2. It shows the DESQview version number, the amount of memory allocated for the Manifest window, and the size and position of the Manifest window.

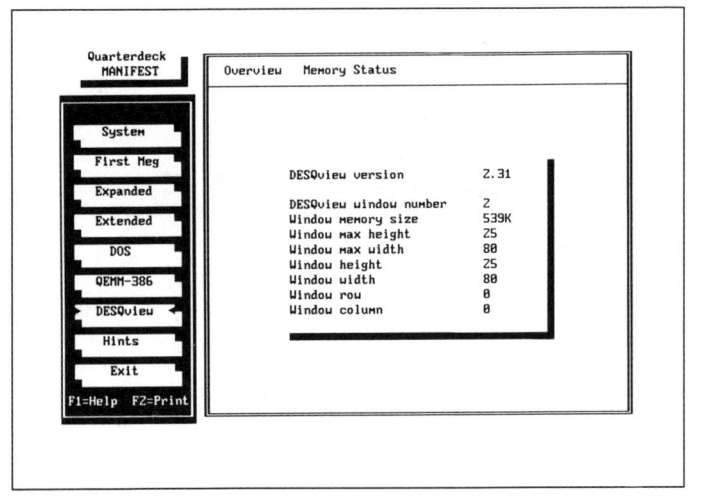

```
Quarterdeck
MANIFEST            Overview   Memory Status

  System

  First Meg
                      DESQview version           2.31
  Expanded
                      DESQview window number     2
  Extended            Window memory size         539K
                      Window max height          25
   DOS                Window max width           80
                      Window height              25
  QEMM-386            Window width               80
                      Window row                 0
  DESQview            Window column              0

  Hints

  Exit

F1=Help  F2=Print
```

Figure IV.2: The Manifest DESQview Overview screen

To Display the DESQview Overview Screen

1. Select the DESQview category.
2. Select the Overview topic.

See Also *DESQview Memory Status*

DOS DRIVERS

- **PURPOSE** Shows a list of the DOS device drivers installed in your system. The display includes information about the standard devices present in all DOS systems, as well as other devices which are loaded from statements in your CONFIG.SYS file.

For all device drivers listed, the device name is shown along with a characteristics map. Standard devices are identified as belonging to DOS. Devices loaded from statements in the CONFIG.SYS file are shown with the memory area they use and their relative size.

To Display the DOS Drivers Screen

1. Select the **DOS** category.
2. Select the Drivers topic.

See Also *DOS Files, DOS Overview*

DOS ENVIRONMENT

- **PURPOSE** Shows information about the DOS environment. It will tell you how much total memory is available and how many

136 Manifest Memory Analyzer

bytes are not used at this point. You will also see the environment variables and their values.

Some of the more common environment variables, as illustrated in Figure IV.3, are *COMSPEC* (where COMMAND.COM is located), the *PATH* (where DOS searches for files), and the *PROMPT* (what the DOS command line prompt looks like).

To Display the DOS Environment Screen

1. Select the **DOS** category.
2. Select the Environment topic.

See Also   *Dos Files, DOS Overview*

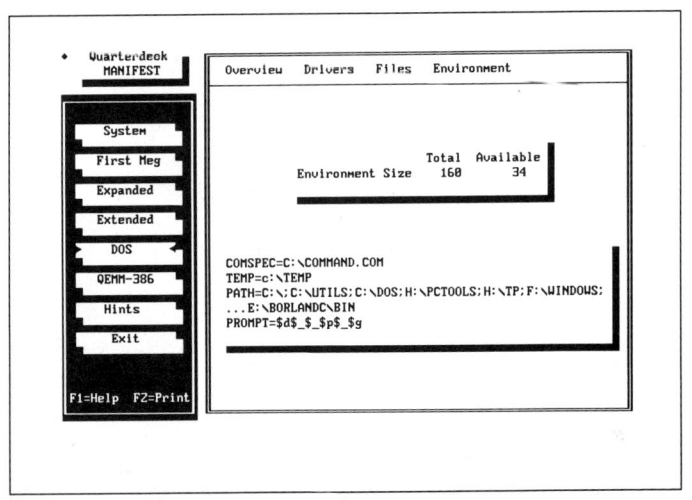

Figure IV.3: The Manifest DOS Environment screen

DOS FILES

- **PURPOSE** Displays the total number of files and file control blocks (FCBS) available, as well as the number currently open. It then lists the names of the open files and FCBS.

To Display the DOS Files Screen

1. Select the **DOS** category.
2. Select the Files topic.

- **NOTES** You can use this screen to determine if you have set up enough Files and FCBS in your CONFIG.SYS file.

See Also *DOS Drivers, DOS Environment, DOS Overview, FCBS.COM* (Part III), *FILES.COM* (Part III)

DOS OVERVIEW

- **PURPOSE** Shows a summary of the memory used by the disk operating system on your computer. It is useful to review this screen to check or confirm the resources of your system. Figure IV.4 illustrates this screen. You can pinpoint excessive resource allocation or check the effect on your system of installing device drivers or buffers in high memory.

To Display the DOS Overview Screen

1. Select the **DOS** category.
2. Select the **O**verview topic.

See Also *DOS Drivers, DOS Environment, DOS Files*

138 Manifest Memory Analyzer

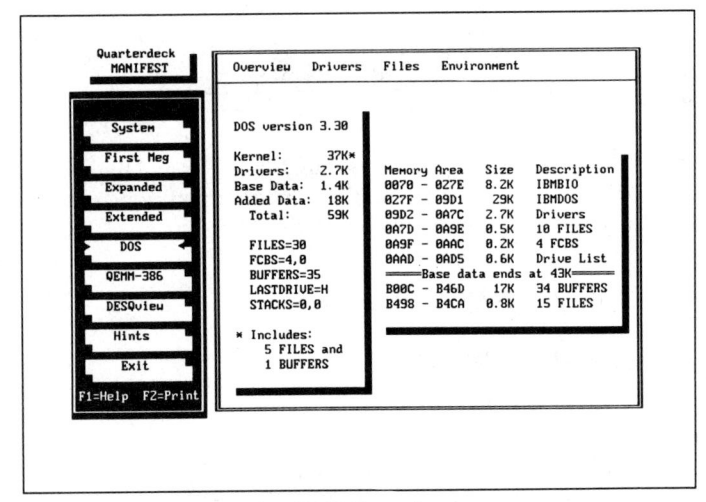

Figure IV.4: The Manifest DOS Overview screen

EXIT EXIT

- **PURPOSE**   Terminates Manifest and returns you to the DOS command line.

To Leave Manifest and Return to DOS

1. Select the Exit category.
2. Select the Exit topic.
3. Press **Esc**.

Shortcut   Press the **Esc** key twice in succession from anywhere in Manifest to leave the program.

See Also   *Exit Stay Resident*

EXIT STAY RESIDENT

- **PURPOSE** Instructs Manifest to run as a terminate-and-stay-resident program (TSR). You can then run some other program and "pop up" Manifest at any time, using a key combination you've specified, to examine the effect the new program has had on your system. The ability to run Manifest as a TSR is important mostly if you're an advanced user trying to track down a specific problem with your software.

To Run Manifest as a TSR

1. Select the Exit category.
2. Select the Stay Resident topic.
3. Specify the key combination you want to use to pop Manifest up by holding down any one of the combinations shown on the screen (illustrated in Figure IV.5).

See Also *Exit Exit*

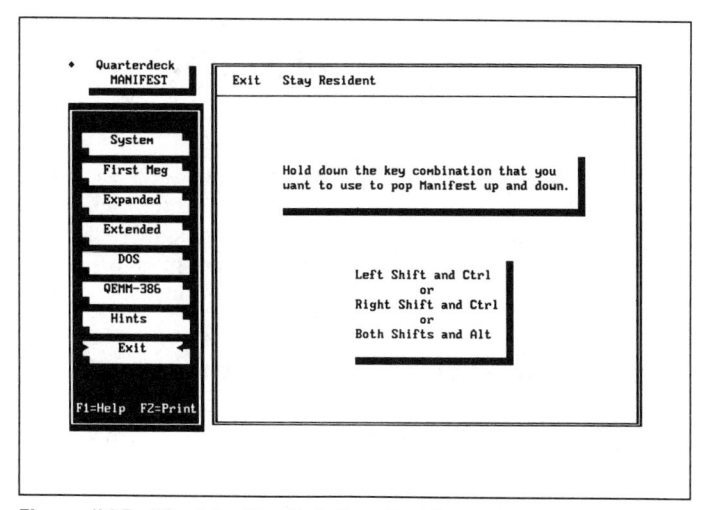

Figure IV.5: The Manifest Exit Stay Resident screen

EXPANDED BENCHMARK

• **PURPOSE**   Tests the speed of your expanded memory manager. Use the results displayed in this screen to compare different memory managers or to determine how quickly interrupts can be handled on your system. The results are measured in microseconds, where one million microseconds is equal to one second. You will see the maximum, minimum, and average times required for the given function. This option will not be displayed if your system does not have expanded memory.

To Display the Expanded Benchmark Screen

1. Select the **Ex**panded category.
2. Select the **B**enchmark topic.

See Also   *Expanded Handles, Expanded Overview, Expanded Pages, Expanded Timings*

EXPANDED HANDLES

• **PURPOSE**   Reports on the currently allocated expanded memory (EMS) handles. For each handle, the display shows the handle number, the amount of memory allocated to it in kilobytes, and any names that might be assigned to it. This option will not be displayed if your system does not have expanded memory.

To Display the Expanded Handles Screen

1. Select the **Ex**panded category.
2. Select the **Ha**ndles topic.

See Also *Expanded Benchmark, Expanded Overview, Expanded Pages, Expanded Timings*

EXPANDED OVERVIEW

- **PURPOSE** Shows the type of expanded memory in your system and the amount of expanded memory that is available.

The Expanded Overview screen has two sections, as illustrated in Figure IV.6. The top section describes general characteristics of your expanded memory, while the lower section describes the memory and other resources managed by the memory manager. This option will not be displayed if your system does not have expanded memory.

To Display the Expanded Overview Screen

1. Select the Expanded category.

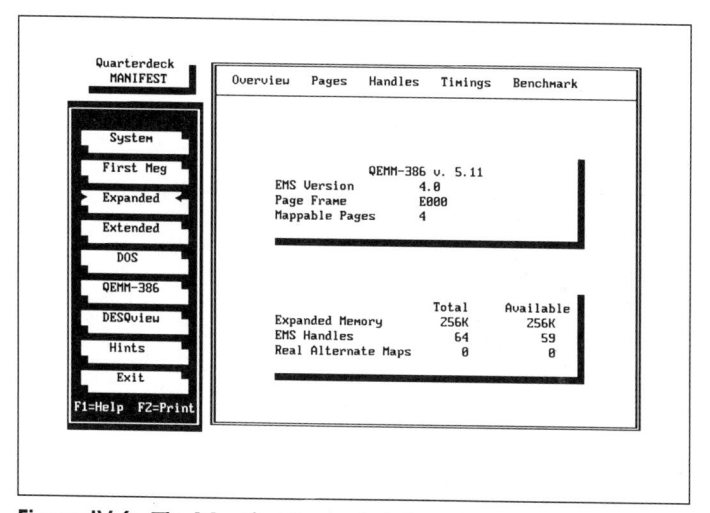

```
                              QEMM-386 v. 5.11
            EMS Version          4.0
            Page Frame           E000
            Mappable Pages       4


                                   Total      Available
            Expanded Memory        256K         256K
            EMS Handles             64           59
            Real Alternate Maps      0            0
```

Figure IV.6: The Manifest Expanded Overview screen

142 Manifest Memory Analyzer

2. Select the Overview topic.

See Also *Expanded Benchmark, Expanded Handles, Expanded Pages, Expanded Timings*

EXPANDED PAGES

- **PURPOSE** Gives details about the first megabyte of memory as it relates to expanded memory in your system. If you're an experienced user, this information will be helpful in confirming installation of memory boards and expanded memory drivers. This option will not be displayed if your system does not have expanded memory.

The vertical table on the left side of the screen, illustrated in Figure IV.7, lists sixteen 64K areas. Each area has four 16K segments marked to indicate expanded memory usage. A legend describing the codes appears at the bottom of the screen next to the table.

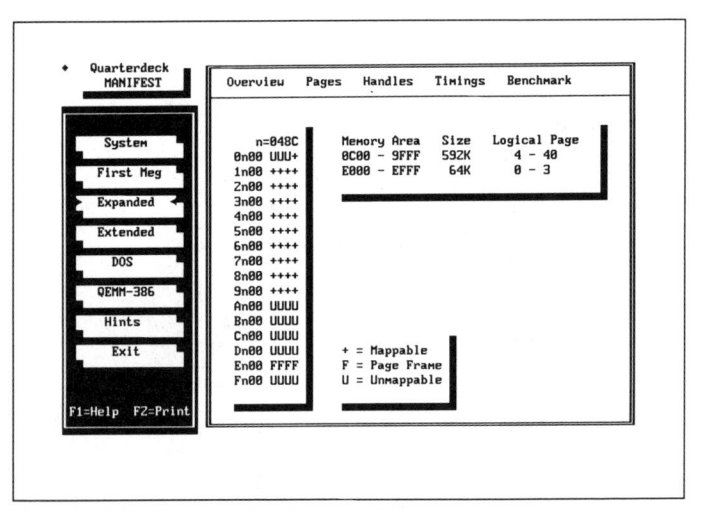

```
•   Quarterdeck
    MANIFEST          Overview  Pages  Handles  Timings  Benchmark

  ┌─────────────┐       n=048C      Memory Area   Size   Logical Page
  │   System    │     0n00 UUU+     0C00 - 9FFF   592K     4 - 40
  ├─────────────┤     1n00 ++++     E000 - EFFF    64K     0 - 3
  │  First Meg  │     2n00 ++++
  ├─────────────┤     3n00 ++++
  │  Expanded ◄ │     4n00 ++++
  ├─────────────┤     5n00 ++++
  │  Extended   │     6n00 ++++
  ├─────────────┤     7n00 ++++
  │    DOS      │     8n00 ++++
  ├─────────────┤     9n00 ++++
  │  QEMM-386   │     An00 UUUU
  ├─────────────┤     Bn00 UUUU
  │   Hints     │     Cn00 UUUU
  ├─────────────┤     Dn00 UUUU    + = Mappable
  │   Exit      │     En00 FFFF    F = Page Frame
  └─────────────┘     Fn00 UUUU    U = Unmappable
  F1=Help F2=Print
```

Figure IV.7: The Manifest Expanded Pages screen

The horizontal table at the top of the screen lists logical page usage, showing the area of memory used, its size, and the number of pages allocated to the area.

To Display the Expanded Pages Screen

1. Select the Expanded category.
2. Select the Pages topic.

See Also *Expanded Benchmark, Expanded Handles, Expanded Overview, Expanded Timings*

EXPANDED TIMINGS

- **PURPOSE** Displays access times for your expanded memory. The purpose of this display is to show how fast the expanded memory in your computer is relative to that of a PC/XT, and to show the relative speeds of different areas of expanded memory.

The amount of memory tested is shown in kilobytes. The speed is calculated in kilobytes per second. The PC index shows the speed of your PC relative to the original PC/XT computer. Also note that, according to Manifest's manual, the results reported here are reliable within 10% each time the screen is displayed. This option will not be displayed if your system does not have expanded memory.

To Display the Expanded Timings Screen

1. Select the Expanded category.
2. Select the Timings topic.

See Also *Expanded Benchmark, Expanded Handles, Expanded Overview, Expanded Pages*

144 Manifest Memory Analyzer

EXTENDED OVERVIEW

- **PURPOSE** Shows you a list of the extended memory in your system. You will see the range of memory addresses used, their size, and whether that memory is free or not.

The list displayed by this command, illustrated in Figure IV.8, reports the area's beginning and ending addresses and its size. The status of the memory refers to the way extended memory is being allocated. Some programs allocate extended memory from the lowest to the highest address first, beginning at 1024K. When memory is allocated in this manner, its status is reported as "Used from the bottom." Other programs allocate extended memory from the top of extended memory downward. When memory is allocated in this manner, its status is labeled "Used from the top."

To Display the Extended Overview Screen

1. Select the Extended category.

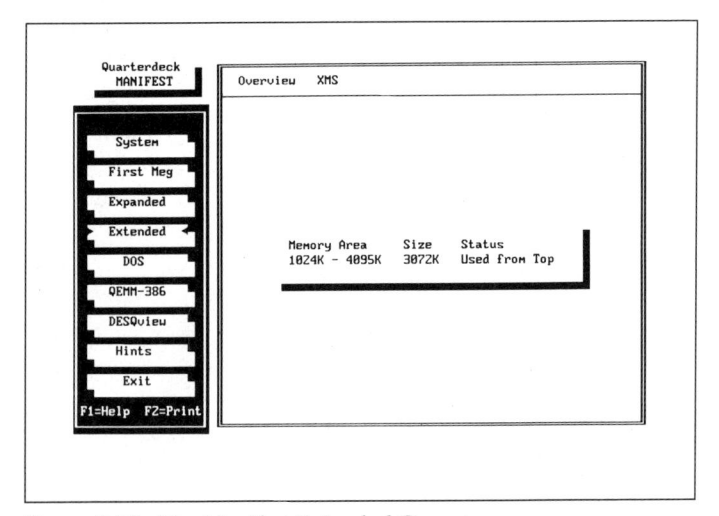

```
Quarterdeck
 MANIFEST         Overview   XMS

  System
 First Meg
 Expanded
 Extended ◄
                  Memory Area    Size    Status
   DOS            1024K - 4095K  3072K   Used from Top
 QEMM-386
 DESQview
   Hints
   Exit
F1=Help F2=Print
```

Figure IV.8: The Manifest Extended Overview screen

2. Select the Overview topic.

See Also *Extended XMS*

EXTENDED XMS

● **PURPOSE** Shows you the XMS support available in your system. If you have applications that use XMS, this screen will help you determine if your XMS capability is sufficient for your needs.

The Extended XMS screen displays specific information about the XMS driver that has been loaded into your system. The top part of the screen shows information about some of the XMS driver's resources. The bottom of the screen shows which XMS memory resources have not yet been used.

In the top part of the screen, you will find the XMS version you are using, the driver revision number, whether high memory has been allocated, whether the A20 hardware address line has been enabled, and the number of handles available for use with XMS memory.

This option is not available if you do not have an XMS driver installed.

To Display the Extended XMS Screen

1. Select the Extended category.
2. Select the XMS topic.

See Also *Extended Overview*

FIRST MEG BIOS DATA

- **PURPOSE** Shows the data area in RAM which is reserved for use by the ROM BIOS. The display consists of several screens. Experienced users will find these screens helpful as a reference to the BIOS data structure and for quick access to port address values.

Many application programs reference, and may change, the information contained in the displayed memory area. The information shown, starting in the first column, is the offset within the BIOS data area, the name or purpose of the data, and the current contents of the memory involved.

To Display the First Meg BIOS Data Screen

1. Select the First Meg category.
2. Select the BIOS Data topic.

See Also *First Meg Interrupts, First Meg Overview, First Meg Programs, First Meg Timings*

FIRST MEG INTERRUPTS

- **PURPOSE** Presents two detailed views on two separate screens of your computer's interrupt vectors, which provide technical information for use by programmers and technical support personnel.

The Interrupts by Owners screen, illustrated in Figure IV.9, lists by address the programs, drivers, and ROMs providing interrupt services, followed by the interrupt numbers they service. The Interrupts by Numbers screen, shown in Figure IV.10, lists the interrupts by number, giving the name or purpose of the interrupt, its address, and the name of the program, driver, or ROM providing the service. Press the **F3** key to switch between screens.

First Meg Interrupts   147

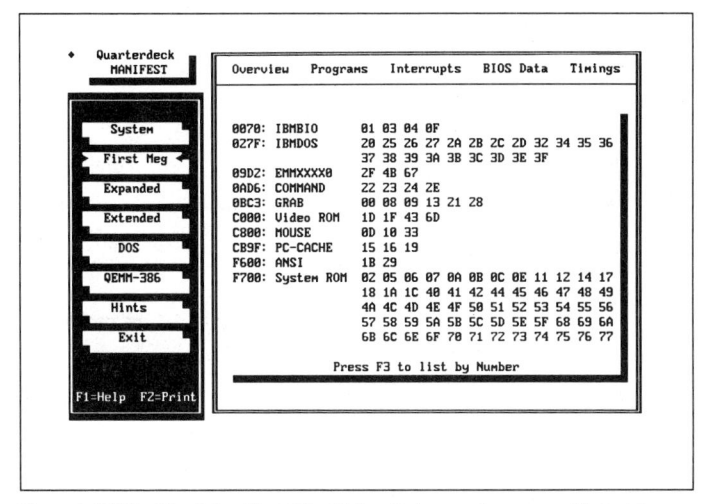

```
 • Quarterdeck
   MANIFEST        Overview   Programs   Interrupts   BIOS Data   Timings

   System          0070: IBMBIO      01 03 04 0F
                   027F: IBMDOS      20 25 26 27 2A 2B 2C 2D 32 34 35 36
   First Meg ◄                       37 38 39 3A 3B 3C 3D 3E 3F
                   09D2: EMMXXXX0    2F 4B 67
   Expanded        0AD6: COMMAND     22 23 24 2E
                   0BC3: GRAB        00 08 09 13 21 28
   Extended        C000: Video ROM   1D 1F 43 6D
                   C800: MOUSE       0D 10 33
   DOS             CB9F: PC-CACHE    15 16 19
                   F600: ANSI        1B 29
   QEMM-386        F700: System ROM  02 05 06 07 0A 0B 0C 0E 11 12 14 17
                                     18 1A 1C 40 41 42 44 45 46 47 48 49
   Hints                             4A 4C 4D 4E 4F 50 51 52 53 54 55 56
                                     57 58 59 5A 5B 5C 5D 5E 5F 68 69 6A
   Exit                              6B 6C 6E 6F 70 71 72 73 74 75 76 77

                               Press F3 to list by Number
 F1=Help  F2=Print
```

Figure IV.9: The Manifest First Meg Interrupts screen (listed by Owner)

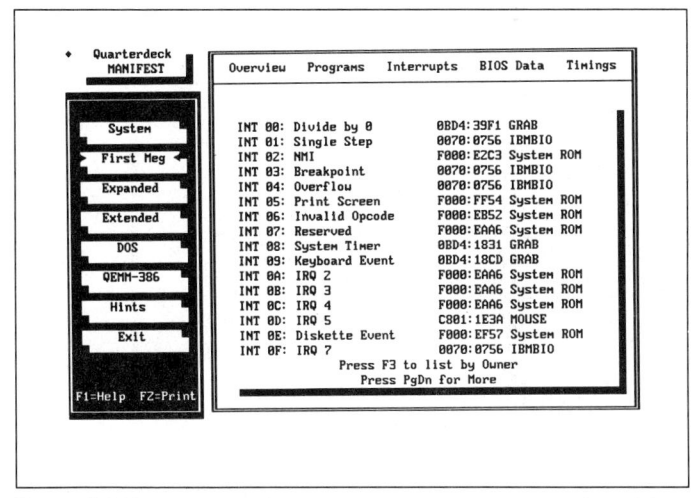

```
 • Quarterdeck
   MANIFEST        Overview   Programs   Interrupts   BIOS Data   Timings

   System          INT 00: Divide by 0         0BD4:39F1 GRAB
                   INT 01: Single Step         0070:0756 IBMBIO
   First Meg ◄     INT 02: NMI                 F000:E2C3 System ROM
                   INT 03: Breakpoint          0070:0756 IBMBIO
   Expanded        INT 04: Overflow            0070:0756 IBMBIO
                   INT 05: Print Screen        F000:FF54 System ROM
   Extended        INT 06: Invalid Opcode      F000:EB52 System ROM
                   INT 07: Reserved            F000:EAA6 System ROM
   DOS             INT 08: System Timer        0BD4:1831 GRAB
                   INT 09: Keyboard Event      0BD4:18CD GRAB
   QEMM-386        INT 0A: IRQ 2               F000:EAA6 System ROM
                   INT 0B: IRQ 3               F000:EAA6 System ROM
   Hints           INT 0C: IRQ 4               F000:EAA6 System ROM
                   INT 0D: IRQ 5               C801:1E3A MOUSE
   Exit            INT 0E: Diskette Event      F000:EF57 System ROM
                   INT 0F: IRQ 7               0070:0756 IBMBIO
                            Press F3 to list by Owner
                            Press PgDn for More
 F1=Help  F2=Print
```

Figure IV.10: The Manifest First Meg Interrupts screen (listed by Number)

148 Manifest Memory Analyzer

To Display the First Meg Interrupts Screen

1. Select the First Meg category.
2. Select the Interrupts topic.

See Also *First Meg BIOS Data, First Meg Overview, First Meg Programs, First Meg Timings*

FIRST MEG OVERVIEW

- **PURPOSE** Displays a list of the memory areas used in the first megabyte of address space on your computer. The information is presented in tabular form, as illustrated in Figure IV.11, giving the area used (expressed in hexadecimal notation), its size in kilobytes, and a description of how that location is being used.

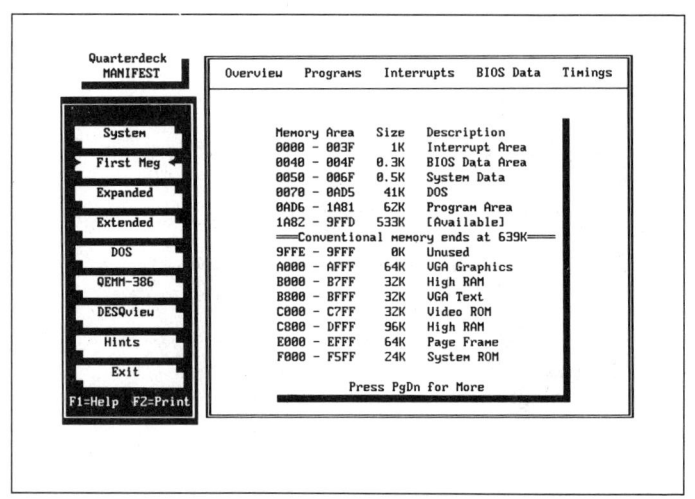

```
Quarterdeck
MANIFEST        Overview  Programs  Interrupts  BIOS Data  Timings

                Memory Area    Size    Description
System          0000 - 003F     1K     Interrupt Area
                0040 - 004F    0.3K    BIOS Data Area
First Meg       0050 - 006F    0.5K    System Data
                0070 - 0AD5    41K     DOS
Expanded        0AD6 - 1A81    62K     Program Area
                1A82 - 9FFD   533K     [Available]
Extended        ═══Conventional memory ends at 639K═══
                9FFE - 9FFF     0K     Unused
DOS             A000 - AFFF    64K     VGA Graphics
                B000 - B7FF    32K     High RAM
QEMM-386        B800 - BFFF    32K     VGA Text
                C000 - C7FF    32K     Video ROM
DESQview        C800 - DFFF    96K     High RAM
                E000 - EFFF    64K     Page Frame
Hints           F000 - F5FF    24K     System ROM

Exit                         Press PgDn for More
F1=Help  F2=Print
```

Figure IV.11: The Manifest First Meg Overview screen

The top part of the display lists your computer's conventional memory below 640K, while the lower part lists high memory (640K to 1024K). If the information takes up more than one page, use the **PgUp** and **PgDn** keys to display all the information.

To Display the First Meg Overview Screen

1. Select the First Meg category.
2. Select the Overview topic.

See Also *First Meg BIOS Data, First Meg Interrupts, First Meg Programs, First Meg Timings*

FIRST MEG PROGRAMS

- **PURPOSE** Displays a list of the programs that are loaded in memory. The memory used by DOS and device drivers is not displayed with this command.

The list identifies the programs that are loaded in conventional memory, the area in memory where they are located, and the amount of memory they take up. If you use QEMM-386, a double line may appear on the display, indicating the point where conventional memory ends and high memory begins.

To Display the First Meg Programs Screen

1. Select the First Meg category.
2. Select the Programs topic.

See Also *First Meg BIOS Data, First Meg Interrupts, First Meg Overview, First Meg Timings*

FIRST MEG TIMINGS

● **PURPOSE**   Reports memory access times for various segments of your computer's first megabyte of memory. The table shows the areas of memory being tested, the access time in kilobytes per second, and a comparative index value, which compares the memory speed relative to a PC/XT computer.

To Display the First Meg Timings Screen

1. Select the First Meg category.
2. Select the Timings topic.

See Also   *First Meg BIOS Data, First Meg Interrupts, First Meg Overview, First Meg Programs*

HELP

● **PURPOSE**   Gives you online assistance in using the Manifest screens. The meaning or purpose of some of the information displayed by Manifest may not be immediately apparent to you. Use the Help screen to interpret the information Manifest provides.

To Display the Help Screen

1. Press the **F1** key.
2. Press **Esc** to exit the Help screen.

HINTS DETAIL

- **PURPOSE** Tells you why Manifest is recommending the modifications to your system shown on the Hints Overview screen. As illustrated in Figure IV.12, it also points out circumstances in which the suggested modification should not be made and instructs you how to make the suggested changes. Use the **PgUp** and **PgDn** keys to move from one Hints Detail screen to another.

To Display the Hints Detail Screen

1. Select the **H**ints category.
2. Select the Detail topic.

See Also *Hints Overview*

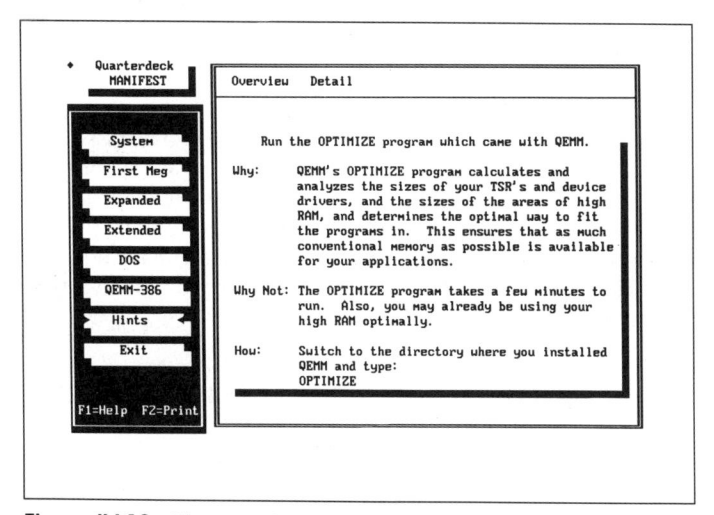

```
    Quarterdeck
    MANIFEST        Overview   Detail

   ┌─────────┐    Run the OPTIMIZE program which came with QEMM.
   │ System  │
   ├─────────┤   Why:    QEMM's OPTIMIZE program calculates and
   │First Meg│            analyzes the sizes of your TSR's and device
   ├─────────┤            drivers, and the sizes of the areas of high
   │Expanded │            RAM, and determines the optimal way to fit
   ├─────────┤            the programs in.  This ensures that as much
   │Extended │            conventional memory as possible is available
   ├─────────┤            for your applications.
   │  DOS    │
   ├─────────┤   Why Not: The OPTIMIZE program takes a few minutes to
   │ QEMM-386│            run.  Also, you may already be using your
   ├─────────┤            high RAM optimally.
   │ Hints   │◄
   ├─────────┤   How:    Switch to the directory where you installed
   │  Exit   │           QEMM and type:
   └─────────┘           OPTIMIZE

 F1=Help F2=Print
```

Figure IV.12: The Manifest Hints Detail screen

HINTS OVERVIEW

- **PURPOSE** Presents you with a list of optimizations you may wish to perform on your system. If Manifest has not found anything on which to comment, the screen will display the message "Everything checks out OK. Nothing to suggest."

To Display the Hints Overview Screen

1. Select the **H**ints category.
2. Select the **O**verview topic.

See Also *Hints Detail*

QEMM-386 ACCESSED

- **PURPOSE** Presents you with a map and a list of your expanded memory. Press **F3** to toggle between the two displays. The map, illustrated in Figure IV.13, shows you blocks of memory that have been accessed since the memory was originally mapped. The list shows multiple blocks of contiguous memory, indicating which have been accessed and which have not. Those that have not been accessed might be available for other uses. This option is displayed only when QEMM-386 is resident in memory.

To Display the QEMM-386 Accessed Screen

1. Select the **Q**EMM-386 category.
2. Select the **A**ccessed topic.

See Also *QEMM-386 Analysis, QEMM-386 Memory, QEMM-386 Overview, QEMM-386 Type*

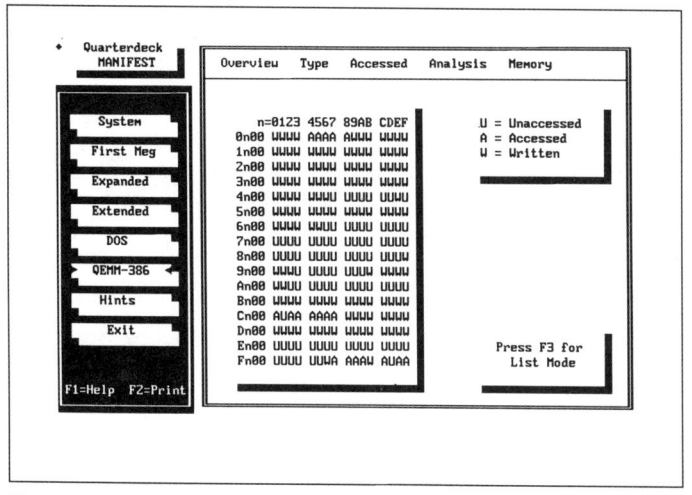

Figure IV.13: The Manifest QEMM-386 Accessed screen (Map mode)

QEMM-386 ANALYSIS

- **PURPOSE** Presents you with two views, in map format and list format, of your computer's first megabyte of memory. The information presented will tell you which areas of memory are OK to use, which areas should be "Excluded," and which should be "Included" using the appropriate QEMM386.SYS parameters in your CONFIG.SYS file.

To Display the QEMM-386 Analysis Screen

1. Select the QEMM-386 category.
2. Select the Analysis topic.

- **NOTES** The information reported will be accurate only if you execute all the programs you usually run and use all the hardware on your computer. See *QEMM.COM ANALYSIS* in Part III for a discussion of the complete procedure.

See Also *QEMM-386 Accessed, QEMM-386 Memory, QEMM-386 Overview, QEMM-386 Type, QEMM.COM ANALYSIS* (Part III)

QEMM-386 MEMORY

- **PURPOSE** Lists the memory in your PC before and after QEMM-386 has configured it.

To Display the QEMM-386 Memory Screen

1. Select the **Q**EMM-386 category.
2. Select the **M**emory topic.

See Also *QEMM-386 Accessed, QEMM-386 Analysis, QEMM-386 Overview, QEMM-386 Type*

QEMM-386 OVERVIEW

- **PURPOSE** Displays the main elements necessary to check QEMM-386's status. See Figure IV.14 for an example. The display will tell you four main points about QEMM: the version of QEMM being used, the status of QEMM, its current mode, and the address of the page frame.

To Display the QEMM-386 Overview Screen

1. Select the **Q**EMM-386 category.
2. Select the **O**verview topic.

QEMM-386 Type   155

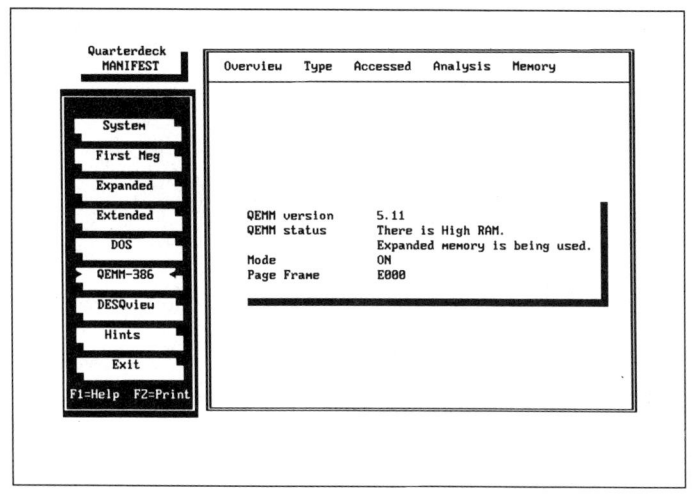

```
 Quarterdeck
  MANIFEST      Overview  Type  Accessed  Analysis  Memory

  System
  First Meg
  Expanded
  Extended       QEMM version    5.11
  DOS            QEMM status     There is High RAM.
                                 Expanded memory is being used.
  QEMM-386       Mode            ON
                 Page Frame      E000
  DESQview
  Hints
  Exit
F1=Help F2=Print
```

Figure IV.14: The Manifest QEMM-386 Overview screen

See Also *QEMM-386 Accessed, QEMM-386 Analysis, QEMM-386 Memory, QEMM-386 Type*

QEMM-386 TYPE

- **PURPOSE** Reports on your computer's expanded memory usage. You can display the information as either a list or a map, pressing **F3** to switch between them. Both displays show how each block of memory in your system is being used.

To Display the QEMM-386 Type Screen

1. Select the **QEMM-386** category.
2. Select the Type topic.

156 Manifest Memory Analyzer

See Also *QEMM-386 Accessed, QEMM-386 Analysis, QEMM-386 Memory, QEMM-386 Overview*

SYSTEM ADAPTERS

● **PURPOSE** Presents several screens of information about your computer's video monitors, adapters, serial ports, parallel ports, and disk drives. If you own an IBM PS/2 computer, Manifest reports information about the special adapters present on this machine.

To Display the System Adapters Screen

1. Select the System category.
2. Select the Adapters topic.

See Also *System AUTOEXEC, System CMOS, System CONFIG, System Overview*

SYSTEM AUTOEXEC

● **PURPOSE** Displays the contents of your computer's AUTOEXEC.BAT batch file , if there is one.

To Display the System AUTOEXEC Screen

1. Select the System category.
2. Select the AUTOEXEC topic.

See Also *System Adapters, System CMOS, System CONFIG, System Overview*

SYSTEM CMOS

- **PURPOSE** Allows you to switch among several screens of information that show you the contents of the CMOS memory in your computer.

To Display the System CMOS Screen

1. Select the System category.
2. Select the CMOS topic.

- **NOTES** The CMOS is a special memory location which stores setup information crucial to the operation of your computer. The information in the CMOS memory is preserved by battery power when you turn your PC off, so it is always kept available.

See Also *System Adapters, System AUTOEXEC, System CONFIG, System Overview*

SYSTEM CONFIG

- **PURPOSE** Displays the contents of your computer's CONFIG.SYS file, if there is one.

To Display the System CONFIG Screen

1. Select the System category.

158 Manifest Memory Analyzer

2. Select the CONFIG topic.

See Also *System Adapters, System AUTOEXEC, System CMOS, System Overview*

SYSTEM OVERVIEW

- **PURPOSE** Tells you about your PC hardware. It will describe your computer's hardware configuration and will print a summary of the hardware features of your computer. Figure IV.1 illustrates the screen.

The upper box describes your computer's hardware configuration. The lower box displays the total amount of conventional, extended, and expanded memory in your computer, as well as the amount of each type of memory currently available for your programs.

To Display the System Overview Screen

1. Select the System category.

2. Select the Overview topic.

See Also *System Adapters, System AUTOEXEC, System CMOS, System CONFIG*

Index

⏎ (Enter key), 5
' (quoting character), 6, 33, 50
? (question mark)
    as LOADHI parameter, 113
    as QEMM.COM parameter, 102
    as QEMM386.SYS parameter, 70
    as VIDRAM parameter, 124

A

accent key (`), 6, 33, 50
adapter RAM, 111
Add a Program command, 12–16
Advanced Setup, 48–52
Alt key, 3, 5, 30
ANSI.SYS file, 27
Applications programs and
       expanded memory, 56
arrow keys, 5–6
ASCII text file format, 21
Auto Dialer command, 16–17, 49–50
AUTOEXEC.BAT file, 68–69,
    120–121, 123, 156–157
AUTO parameter
    QEMM.COM, 106
    QEMM386.SYS, 72

B

Backspace key, 6
baud rate, 49

Big DOS, 18
    DOS Services command and, 26
    Setup command and, 47, 48
BIOS data
    Manifest, 146
    extended, 92–93
BUFFERS.COM, 68, 120
buffers for scripts, 33, 50, 56

C

Change a Program command, 19–20
Change Colors command, 18–19
Close Window command, 4, 20–21
colors, screen, 18–19, 44, 50, 57
common memory, 35
Compaq disable feature, 85
COMPAQEGAROM parameter,
    73–74. *See also* QEMM386.SYS
COMPAQHALFROM parameter,
    74. *See also* QEMM386.SYS
COMPAQROMMEMORY
    parameter, 74–75. *See also*
    QEMM386.SYS
COMPAQ386S parameter, 72–73.
    See also QEMM386.SYS
CONFIG.SYS file, 27, 68–69,
    120–123, 157–158. *See also*
    QEMM386.SYS
conventional memory, 8, 35, 68, 111,
    149
    LOADHI LO and, 116
    QEMM.COM ANALYSIS and,
        105–106

QEMM.COM MEMORY and, 107–108
QEMM386.SYS NOFILL and, 86–87
Convert a Script command, 21–22
Ctrl-Alt-Del key combination, 5
Ctrl-Break key combination, 6, 32
Ctrl-End key combination, 6
Ctrl key, 5
Ctrl-NumLock key combination, 5
Ctrl-Shift-Del key combination, 5

D

Delete a Program command, 22–23
Delete key, 6
Deleting scripts, 33–34
DESQ key, 3, 5
DESQview-specific programs, 6–7, 12–15, 58
device driver, 27
dialing, 16–17
direct memory access (DMA), 76, 83–84
directories, sorting, 24–25
displaying list of scripts, 32
DOS access from DESQview, 23–26
DOS Resource programs, 68, 120–123
DOS Services command, 23–26
 Big DOS and, 26
 options within, 25–26
DVANSI command, 27
DVSETUP command, 47–48
DV.COM program, 2
DV.EXE program, 2

E

EMS2EXT.SYS, 128–129
editing scripts, 33
End key, 6
Enter (↵) key, 5
Esc key, 6
expanded memory (EMS), 8–9, 35, 68, 108, 111, 152–153
 for applications programs, 56
 handles, 80–81, 140–143
 QEMM.COM OFF and, 109
 QEMM.COM ON and, 109
 QEMM386.SYS DOS4 and, 76
 QEMM386.SYS FORCEEMS and, 78–79
 QEMM386.SYS NOEMS and, 86
 QEMM386.SYS OFF and, 94
 QEMM386.SYS ON and, 95
 speed of, 140, 143
extended BIOS data area, 92–93
extended memory (XMS), 8–9, 68, 108, 144–145
 EMS2EXT.SYS and, 128–129
 QEMM386.SYS EMBMEM and, 77
 QEMM386.SYS EXTMEM and, 78
 QEMM386.SYS MEMORY and, 84–85

QEMM386.SYS NOXMS and, 93–94
QEMM386.SYS UNUSUALEXT and, 99–100
extended memory blocks (EMB), 8–9

F

FCBS.COM, 68, 121
FILES.COM, 68, 122
Fixed-Size Pause, 34
Freeze command, 4, 27–28

G

global scripts, 30–32

H

handles, 80–81, 140–143
handles summary, Manifest, 140–141
Help command, 28–29
help features, Manifest, 150
HELP parameter
    LOADHI, 116
    QEMM.COM, 107
    QEMM386.SYS, 81
    VIDRAM, 124–125
Hide command, 4, 29
high memory, 8, 108, 149

high memory area (HMA), 8–9, 81–82, 87
high RAM, 8, 111–112, 116
Home key, 6

I

ill-behaved programs, 10, 58
Insert key, 6
interrupts, 56, 98, 146–148

K

keyboard controller, 98–99

L

largest available memory, 36, 112–114
LASTDRIVE.COM, 68, 122–123
Learn feature, 30–34
Learn key, 5, 30
Learn script, 21–22
LOADHI, 96–97, 112–119
    ? parameter, 113
    BESTFIT parameter, 113
    EXCLUDELARGEST parameter, 114
    EXCLUDEREGION parameter, 114
    EXCLUDESMALLEST parameter, 114–115

GETSIZE parameter, 115
HAPPIEST parameter, 115
HELP parameter, 116
LARGEST parameter, 116
LO parameter, 116
NOLO parameter, 116
NOPAUSEONERROR parameter, 117
PAUSE parameter, 117–118
REGION parameter, 118
SIZE parameter, 118
SMALLEST parameter, 119
TERMINATERESIDENT parameter, 119
LOADHI.COM, 68, 112
LOADHI.SYS, 68, 112
loading DESQview, 2
logical drives, 50

M

macro. *See* Learn feature
Manifest, 7, 131–133. *See also* QEMM.COM
 BIOS data, 146
 CMOS data, 157
 DESQview features summary, 134–135
 DOS device summary, 135
 DOS environment summary, 135–136
 DOS files summary, 137
 DOS memory usage analysis, 137–138
 expanded memory analysis, 140–143, 152–156
 expanded memory manager speed analysis, 140, 143
 extended memory analysis, 144–145
 first megabyte memory analysis, 148–150
 handles summary, 140–141
 hardware analysis, 158
 help features, 150
 interrupts data, 146–148
 memory status summary, 133–134
 optimization recommendations, 151–152
 peripherals analysis, 156
 TSR feature, 139
mappable memory, 7, 83, 111
mapped key, 7, 30
mapped ROM, 111
mapping, 7
maps, 7, 84
Mark command, 34, 60
math coprocessor, 57
memory, 8–10
 common, 35
 conventional, 8, 35, 68, 111, 149. *See also* conventional memory
 DMA, 76, 83–84
 EMS, 8–9, 35, 68, 108, 111, 152–153. *See also* expanded memory
 XMS, 8–9, 68, 108, 144–145. *See also* extended memory
 high, 8, 108, 149
 HMA, 8–9, 81–82, 87
 largest available, 36, 112–114
 mappable, 7, 83, 111
 measurement of access to, 103–104
 rammable, 111
 sorting by speed, 90
 top, 91, 108
 total, 36

total available, 36
UMB, 8–9
MEMORY parameter
 QEMM.COM, 107–108
 QEMM386.SYS, 84–85
Memory Status command, 35–36
menus in DESQview, 2–3
Microsoft Windows 3, 10, 92–93
modems, 17, 49–50
mouse, 50–51
MOUSE.COM, 50–51
MOUSE.SYS, 50–51
Move command, 4, 37

N

NOPAUSEONERROR parameter, 117
 LOADHI, 117
 QEMM.COM, 108–109
 QEMM386.SYS, 87–88
 VIDRAM, 126

O

OFF parameter
 QEMM.COM, 109
 QEMM386.SYS, 94
 VIDRAM, 126
ON parameter
 QEMM.COM, 109
 QEMM386.SYS, 95
 VIDRAM, 126–127
Open Window command, 4, 12, 38
OPTIMIZE, 69

P

page frame, 111
Pause key, 5
PAUSE parameter
 LOADHI, 117–118
 QEMM.COM, 109–110
 QEMM386.SYS, 96
 VIDRAM, 127
pausing within scripts, 34
Position command, 39–41
Print-Screen key, 5
program scripts, 30–32
Put Aside command, 42

Q

QEMM.COM, 102. *See also* Manifest
 ? parameter, 102
 ACCESSED MAP parameter, 7, 84, 104
 ACCESSED parameter, 103–104
 ANALYSIS MAP parameter, 7, 84, 106
 ANALYSIS parameter, 105–106
 AUTO parameter, 106
 HELP parameter, 107
 MAP parameter, 107
 MEMORY parameter, 107–108
 NOPAUSEONERROR parameter, 108–109
 OFF parameter, 109
 ON parameter, 109
 PAUSE parameter, 109–110
 RESET parameter, 110
 SUMMARY parameter, 110
 TYPE MAP parameter, 7, 84, 111–112

TYPE parameter, 110–111
QEMM386.SYS, 67–70
  ? parameter, 70
  ADAPTERRAM parameter, 70–71
  ADAPTERROM parameter, 71–72
  AUTO parameter, 72
  COMPAQEGAROM parameter, 73–74
  COMPAQHALFROM parameter, 74
  COMPAQROMMEMORY parameter, 74–75
  COMPAQ386S parameter, 72–73
  DISKBUF parameter, 75
  DMA parameter, 76
  DOS4 parameter, 76–77
  EMBMEM parameter, 77
  EXCLUDE parameter, 77–78, 105, 111
  EXTMEM parameter, 78
  FORCEEMS parameter, 78–79
  FRAMELENGTH parameter, 80
  FRAME parameter, 79
  HANDLES parameter, 80–81
  HELP parameter, 81
  HMAMIN parameter, 81–82
  IGNOREA20 parameter, 82
  INCLUDE parameter, 83, 106
  LOCKDMA parameter, 83–84
  MAPS parameter, 84
  MEMORY parameter, 84–85
  NOCOMPAQFEATURES parameter, 85
  NOEMS parameter, 86
  NOFILL parameter, 86–87
  NOHMA parameter, 87
  NOPAUSEONERROR parameter, 87–88
  NOROMHOLES, 88–89
  NOROM parameter, 88
  NOSHADOWRAM parameter, 89–90
  NOSORT parameter, 90
  NOTOPMEMORY parameter, 91
  NOVIDEOFILL parameter, 91–92
  NOVIDEORAM parameter, 92
  NOWINDOWS3 parameter, 92–93
  NOXBDA parameter, 93
  NOXMS parameter, 93–94
  OFF parameter, 94
  OLDDV parameter, 95
  ON parameter, 95
  PAUSE parameter, 96
  RAM parameter, 96–97
  ROM parameter, 97–98
  TASKS parameter, 98
  UNUSUALEXT parameter, 99–100
  UNUSUAL8042 parameter, 98–99
  VIDRAMEGA parameter, 100
  VIDRAMEMS parameter, 100–101
  WATCHDOG parameter, 101
Quit DESQview command, 42–43
quoting character (`), 6, 33, 50

R

RAM disk, 78
RAM (random access memory), 111–112, 116
  adapter, 111
  shadow, 89–90, 108

rammable memory, 111
Rearrange command, 43–44
remapping, 7
Resize command, 4, 44–45
ROM holes, 88–89
ROM mapping, 97–98

S

Scissors command, 34, 45–46, 61
scripts, 30–34
    buffers for, 33, 50, 56
    deleting, 33–34
    displaying list of, 32
    editing, 33
    global, 30–32
    pausing within, 34
    program, 30–32
    startup, 34
Scroll command, 4, 46–47
Setup DESQview command, 47–52
    Advanced Setup, 48–52
    Simple Setup, 47–48
shadow RAM, 89–90, 108
Shift-DESQ key combination, 5, 30
Shift-Tab key combination, 5
Simple Setup, 47–48
spacebar, 5
Specify Program Information command, 52–58
    advanced options within, 55–58
    options within, 53–55
split ROM, 111
startup scripts, 34

Switch Windows command, 4, 59

T

Tab key, 5
telephone number format, 17, 49
terminate-and-stay-resident programs, 8, 68, 119
Time Delay, 34
top memory, 91, 108
total available memory, 36
total memory, 36
Transfer command, 34, 60–61
TSRs. *See* terminate-and-stay-resident programs
Tune Performance command, 44, 51, 61–63

U

upper memory blocks (UMB), 8–9

V

Variable Pause, 34
video memory, 91–92, 111. *See also* VIDRAM
video modes, 44, 51–52, 63–64

Video Options command, 63–64
VIDRAM, 123–128
  ? parameter, 124
  HELP parameter, 124–125
  NOCGA parameter, 125
  NOEGA parameter, 125
  NOPAUSEONERROR
    parameter, 126
  OFF parameter, 126
  ON parameter, 126–127
  PAUSE parameter, 127
  RESIDENT parameter, 127
  VIDRAMEGA parameter, 128
  VIDRAMEMS parameter, 128
VIDRAM.COM, 68
VIDRAMEGA parameter
  QEMM386.SYS, 100
  VIDRAM, 128
VIDRAMEMS parameter
  QEMM386.SYS, 100–101
  VIDRAM, 128

W

well-behaved programs, 10
windows, 4
  background, 4
  moving, 4, 37
  moving information between,
    4–5, 45–46, 60–61
  position of, 52
  switching, 4, 59

Z

Zoom command, 64–65

Selections from The SYBEX Library

OPERATING SYSTEMS

The ABC's of DOS 4
Alan R. Miller
275pp. Ref. 583-2
This step-by-step introduction to using DOS 4 is written especially for beginners. Filled with simple examples, *The ABC's of DOS 4* covers the basics of hardware, software, disks, the system editor EDLIN, DOS commands, and more.

**ABC's of MS-DOS
(Second Edition)**
Alan R. Miller
233pp. Ref. 493-3
This handy guide to MS-DOS is all many PC users need to manage their computer files, organize floppy and hard disks, use EDLIN, and keep their computers organized. Additional information is given about utilities like Sidekick, and there is a DOS command and program summary. The second edition is fully updated for Version 3.3.

DOS Assembly Language Programming
Alan R. Miller
365pp. 487-9
This book covers PC-DOS through 3.3, and gives clear explanations of how to assemble, link, and debug 8086, 8088, 80286, and 80386 programs. The example assembly language routines are valuable for students and programmers alike.

**DOS Instant Reference
SYBEX Prompter Series**
**Greg Harvey
Kay Yarborough Nelson**
220pp. Ref. 477-1, 4 3/4" × 8"
A complete fingertip reference for fast, easy on-line help:command summaries, syntax, usage and error messages. Organized by function—system commands, file commands, disk management, directories, batch files, I/O, networking, programming, and more. Through Version 3.3.

Encyclopedia DOS
Judd Robbins
1030pp. Ref. 699-5
A comprehensive reference and user's guide to all versions of DOS through 4.0. Offers complete information on every DOS command, with all possible switches and parameters—plus examples of effective usage. An invaluable tool.

**Essential OS/2
(Second Edition)**
Judd Robbins
445pp. Ref. 609-X
Written by an OS/2 expert, this is the guide to the powerful new resources of the OS/2 operating system standard edition 1.1 with presentation manager. Robbins introduces the standard edition, and details multitasking under OS/2, and the range of commands for installing, starting up, configuring, and running applications. For Version 1.1 Standard Edition.

**Essential PC-DOS
(Second Edition)**
**Myril Clement Shaw
Susan Soltis Shaw**
332pp. Ref. 413-5
An authoritative guide to PC-DOS, including version 3.2. Designed to make experts out of beginners, it explores everything from disk management to batch file programming. Includes an 85-page command summary. Through Version 3.2.

Graphics Programming Under Windows
**Brian Myers
Chris Doner**
646pp. Ref. 448-8
Straightforward discussion, abundant examples, and a concise reference guide to graphics commands make this book a must for Windows programmers. Topics range from how Windows works to programming for business, animation, CAD, and desktop publishing. For Version 2.

Hard Disk Instant Reference
SYBEX Prompter Series
Judd Robbins
256pp. Ref. 587-5, 4 ¾" × 8"
Compact yet comprehensive, this pocket-sized reference presents the essential information on DOS commands used in managing directories and files, and in optimizing disk configuration. Includes a survey of third-party utility capabilities. Through DOS 4.0.

Inside DOS: A Programmer's Guide
Michael J. Young
490pp. Ref. 710-X
A collection of practical techniques (with source code listings) designed to help you take advantage of the rich resources intrinsic to MS-DOS machines. Designed for the experienced programmer with a basic understanding of C and 8086 assembly language, and DOS fundamentals.

Mastering DOS (Second Edition)
Judd Robbins
722pp. Ref. 555-7
"The most useful DOS book." This seven-part, in-depth tutorial addresses the needs of users at all levels. Topics range from running applications, to managing files and directories, configuring the system, batch file programming, and techniques for system developers. Through Version 4.

MS-DOS Power User's Guide, Volume I (Second Edition)
Jonathan Kamin
482pp. Ref. 473-9
A fully revised, expanded edition of our best-selling guide to high-performance DOS techniques and utilities—with details on Version 3.3. Configuration, I/O, directory structures, hard disks, RAM disks, batch file programming, the ANSI.SYS device driver, more. Through Version 3.3.

Understanding DOS 3.3
Judd Robbins
678pp. Ref. 648-0
This best selling, in-depth tutorial addresses the needs of users at all levels with many examples and hands-on exercises. Robbins discusses the fundamentals of DOS, then covers manipulating files and directories, using the DOS editor, printing, communicating, and finishes with a full section on batch files.

Understanding Hard Disk Management on the PC
Jonathan Kamin
500pp. Ref. 561-1
This title is a key productivity tool for all hard disk users who want efficient, error-free file management and organization. Includes details on the best ways to conserve hard disk space when using several memory-guzzling programs. Through DOS 4.

Up & Running with Your Hard Disk
Klaus M Rubsam
140pp. Ref. 666-9
A far-sighted, compact introduction to hard disk installation and basic DOS use. Perfect for PC users who want the practical essentials in the shortest possible time. In 20 basic steps, learn to choose your hard disk, work with accessories, back up data, use DOS utilities to save time, and more.

Up & Running with Windows 286/386
Gabriele Wentges
132pp. Ref. 691-X
This handy 20-step overview gives PC users all the essentials of using Windows—whether for evaluating the software, or getting a fast start. Each self-contained lesson takes just 15 minutes to one hour to complete.

UTILITIES

Mastering the Norton Utilities 5
Peter Dyson
400pp, Ref. 725-8
This complete guide to installing and using the Norton Utilities 5 is a must for beginning and experienced users alike. It offers a clear, detailed description of each utility, with options, uses and examples—so users can quickly identify the programs they need and put Norton right to work. Includes valuable coverage of the newest Norton enhancements.

Mastering PC Tools Deluxe 6
For Versions 5.5 and 6.0
425pp. Ref. 700-2
An up-to-date guide to the lifesaving utilities in PC Tools Deluxe version 6.0 from installation, to high-speed back-ups, data recovery, file encryption, desktop applications, and more. Includes detailed background on DOS and hardware such as floppies, hard disks, modems and fax cards.

Mastering SideKick Plus
Gene Weisskopf
394pp. Ref. 558-1
Employ all of Sidekick's powerful and expanded features with this hands-on guide to the popular utility. Features include comprehensive and detailed coverage of time management, note taking, outlining, auto dialing, DOS file management, math, and copy-and-paste functions.

Up & Running with Norton Utilities
Rainer Bartel
140pp. Ref. 659-6
Get up and running in the shortest possible time in just 20 lessons or "steps." Learn to restore disks and files, use UnErase, edit your floppy disks, retrieve lost data and more. Or use the book to evaluate the software before you purchase. Through Version 4.2.

Up & Running with PC Tools Deluxe 6
Thomas Holste
180pp. Ref.678-2
Learn to use this software program in just 20 basic steps. Readers get a quick, inexpensive introduction to using the Tools for disaster recovery, disk and file management, and more.

COMMUNICATIONS

Mastering Crosstalk XVI
(Second Edition)
Peter W. Gofton
225pp. Ref. 642-1
Introducing the communications program Crosstalk XVI for the IBM PC. As well as providing extensive examples of command and script files for programming Crosstalk, this book includes a detailed description of how to use the program's more advanced features, such as windows, talking to mini or mainframe, customizing the keyboard and answering calls and background mode.

Mastering PROCOMM PLUS
Bob Campbell
400pp. Ref. 657-X
Learn all about communications and information retrieval as you master and use PROCOMM PLUS. Topics include choosing and using a modem; automatic dialing; using on-line services (featuring CompuServe) and more. Through Version 1.1b; also covers PROCOMM, the "shareware" version.

Mastering Serial Communications
Peter W. Gofton
289pp. Ref. 180-2
The software side of communications, with details on the IBM PC's serial programming, the XMODEM and Kermit protocols, non-ASCII data transfer, interrupt-level programming and more. Sample programs in C, assembly language and BASIC.

NETWORKS

The ABC's of Local Area Networks
Michael Dortch
212pp. Ref. 664-2
This jargon-free introduction to LANs is for current and prospective users who see general information, comparative options, a look at the future, and tips for effective LANs use today. With comparisons of Token-Ring, PC Network, Novell, and others.

The ABC's of Novell Netware
Jeff Woodward
282pp. Ref. 614-6
For users who are new to PC's or networks, this entry-level tutorial outlines each basic element and operation of Novell. The ABC's introduces computer hardware and software, DOS, network organization and security, and printing and communicating over the netware system.

Mastering Novell Netware
Cheryl C. Currid
Craig A. Gillett
500pp. Ref. 630-8

This book is a thorough guide for System Administrators to installing and operating a microcomputer network using Novell Netware. Mastering covers actually setting up a network from start to finish, design, administration, maintenance, and troubleshooting.

LANGUAGES

The ABC's of GW-BASIC
William R. Orvis
320pp. Ref. 663-4

Featuring two parts: Part I is an easy-to-follow tutorial for beginners, while Part II is a complete, concise reference guide to GW-BASIC commands and functions. Covers everything from the basics of programming in the GW-BASIC environment, to debugging a major program. Includes special treatment of graphics and sound.

The ABC's of Quick C
Douglas Hergert
309pp. Ref. 557-3

This is the most unintimidating C language tutorial, designed especially for readers who have had little or no computer programming experience. The reader will learn programming essentials with step-by-step instructions for working with numbers, strings, arrays, pointers, structures, decisions, and loops. For Version 2.0.

BASIC Programs for Scientists and Engineers
Alan R. Miller
318pp. Ref. 073-3

The algorithms presented in this book are programmed in standard BASIC code which should be usable with almost any implementation of BASIC. Includes statistical calculations, matrix algebra, curve fitting, integration, and more.

FORTRAN Programs for Scientists and Engineers (Second Edition)
Alan R. Miller
280pp. Ref. 571-9

In this collection of widely used scientific algorithms—for statistics, vector and matrix operations, curve fitting, and more—the author stresses effective use of little-known and powerful features of FORTRAN.

Introduction to Pascal: Including Turbo Pascal (Second Edition)
Rodnay Zaks
464pp. Ref. 533-6

This best-selling tutorial builds complete mastery of Pascal—from basic structured programming concepts, to advanced I/O, data structures, file operations, sets, pointers and lists, and more. Both ISO Standard and Turbo Pascal.

Mastering C
Craig Bolon
437pp. Ref. 326-0

This in-depth guide stresses planning, testing, efficiency and portability in C applications. Topics include data types, storage classes, arrays, pointers, data structures, control statements, I/O and the C function library.

Mastering QuickBASIC
Rita Belserene
450pp. Ref. 589-1

Readers build professional programs with this extensive language tutorial. Fundamental commands are mixed with the author's tips and tricks so that users can create their own applications. Program templates are included for video displays, computer games, and working with databases and printers. For Version 4.5.

Mastering QuickC
Stan Kelly-Bootle
602pp. Ref. 550-6

This extensive tutorial covers C language programming and features the latest version of QuickC. Veteran author Kelly-Bootle uses many examples to explain language and style, covering data types, storage classes, file I/O, the Graphics Toolbox, and the window-oriented debugger. For Version 2.0.

Mastering QuickPascal
Michael Yester
581pp. Ref. 653-7

Ideal for QuickPascal programmers who want a general reference to the language, as well as for experience Turbo Pascal programmers who are interested in how object-oriented programming can be used. Includes a complete tutorial on the Pascal language.

Mastering Turbo C (Second Edition)
Stan Kelly-Bootle
609pp. Ref. 595-6
With a foreword by Borland International President Philippe Kahn, this new edition has been expanded to include full details on Version 2.0. Learn theory and practical programming, with tutorials on data types, real numbers and characters, controlling program flow, file I/O, and producing color charts and graphs. Through Version 2.

Mastering Turbo Pascal 6
Scott D. Palmer
650pp, Ref. 675-8
This step-by-step guide to the newest Turbo Pascal release takes readers from programming basics to advanced techniques such as graphics, recursion, object-oriented programming, efficient debugging, and programming for other environments such as Vax/VMS. Includes dozens of useful exercises and examples, and tips for effective programming.

Systems Programming in Microsoft C
Michael J. Young
604pp. Ref. 570-0
This sourcebook of advanced C programming techniques is for anyone who wants to make the most of their C compiler or Microsoft QuickC. It includes a comprehensive, annotated library of systems functions, ready to compile and call.

Turbo Pascal Toolbox (Second Edition)
Frank Dutton
425pp. Ref. 602-2
This collection of tested, efficient Turbo Pascal building blocks gives a boost to intermediate-level programmers, while teaching effective programming by example. Topics include accessing DOS, menus, bit maps, screen handling, and much more.

DATABASES

The ABC's of dBASE III PLUS
Robert Cowart
264pp. Ref. 379-1
The most efficient way to get beginners up and running with dBASE. Every 'how' and 'why' of database management is demonstrated through tutorials and practical dBASE III PLUS applications.

The ABC's of dBASE IV 1.1
Robert Cowart
350pp, Ref. 632-4
The latest version of dBASE IV is featured in this hands-on introduction. It assumes no previous experience with computers or database management, and uses easy-to-follow lessons to introduce the concepts, build basic skills, and set up some practical applications. Includes report writing and Query by Example.

The ABC's of Paradox 3.5 (Second Edition)
Charles Siegel
334pp, Ref. 785-1
This easy-to-follow, hands-on tutorial is a must for beginning users of Paradox 3.0 and 3.5. Even if you've never used a computer before, you'll be doing useful work in just a few short lessons. A clear introduction to database management and valuable business examples make this a "right-to-work" guide for the practical-minded.

Advanced Techniques in dBASE III PLUS
Alan Simpson
454pp. Ref. 369-4
A full course in database design and structured programming, with routines for inventory control, accounts receivable, system management, and integrated databases.

dBASE Instant Reference SYBEX Prompter Series
Alan Simpson
471pp. Ref. 484-4; 4 ¾" × 8"
Comprehensive information at a glance: a brief explanation of syntax and usage for every dBASE command, with step-by-step instructions and exact keystroke sequences. Commands are grouped by function in twenty precise categories.

dBASE III PLUS Programmer's Reference Guide
SYBEX Ready Reference Series
Alan Simpson

1056pp. Ref. 508-5

Programmers will save untold hours and effort using this comprehensive, well-organized dBASE encyclopedia. Complete technical details on commands and functions, plus scores of often-needed algorithms.

dBASE IV 1.1 Programmer's Instant Reference (Second Edition)
Alan Simpson

555pp, Ref. 764-9

Enjoy fast, easy access to information often hidden in cumbersome documentation. This handy pocket-sized reference presents information on each command and function in the dBASE IV programming language. Commands are grouped according to their purpose, so readers can locate the correct command for any task—quickly and easily.

dBASE IV User's Instant Reference (Second Edition)
Alan Simpson

356pp, Ref. 786-X

Completely revised to cover the new 1.1 version of dBASE IV, this handy reference guide presents information on every dBASE operation a user can perform. Exact keystroke sequences are presented, and complex tasks are explained step-by-step. It's a great way for newer users to look up the basics, while more experienced users will find it a fast way to locate information on specialized tasks.

Mastering dBASE III PLUS: A Structured Approach
Carl Townsend

342pp. Ref. 372-4

In-depth treatment of structured programming for custom dBASE solutions. An ideal study and reference guide for applications developers, new and experienced users with an interest in efficient programming.

Mastering dBASE IV Programming
Carl Townsend

496pp. Ref. 540-9

This task-oriented book introduces structured dBASE IV programming and commands by setting up a general ledger system, an invoice system, and a quotation management system. The author carefully explores the unique character of dBASE IV based on his in-depth understanding of the program.

Mastering FoxPro
Charles Seigel

639pp. Ref. 671-5

This guide to the powerful FoxPro DBMS offers a tutorial on database basics, then enables the reader to master new skills and features as needed—with many examples from business. An in-depth tutorial guides users through the development of a complete mailing list system.

Mastering Paradox 3.5
Alan Simpson

650pp, Ref. 677-4

This indispensable, in-depth guide has again been updated for the latest Paradox release, offering the same comprehensive, hands-on treatment featured in highly praised previous editions. It covers everything from database basics to PAL programming—including complex queries and reports, and multi-table applications.

Mastering Q & A (Second Edition)
Greg Harvey

540pp. Ref. 452-6

This hands-on tutorial explores the Q & A Write, File, and Report modules, and the Intelligent Assistant. English-language command processor, macro creation, interfacing with other software, and more, using practical business examples.

Power User's Guide to R:BASE
Alan Simpson
Cheryl Currid
Craig Gillett

446pp. Ref. 354-6

Supercharge your R:BASE applications with this straightforward tutorial that covers system design, structured programming, managing multiple data tables, and more. Sample applications include ready-to-run mailing, inventory and accounts receivable systems. Through Version 2.11.

Understanding dBASE III
Alan Simpson
300pp. Ref. 267-1
dBASE commands and concepts are illustrated throughout with practical, business oriented examples—for mailing list handling, accounts receivable, and inventory design. Contains scores of tips and techniques for maximizing efficiency and meeting special needs.

Understanding dBASE III PLUS
Alan Simpson
415pp. Ref. 349-X
A solid sourcebook of training and ongoing support. Everything from creating a first database to command file programming is presented in working examples, with tips and techniques you won't find anywhere else.

Understanding dBASE IV 1.1
Alan Simpson
900pp, Ref. 633-2
Simpson's outstanding introduction to dBASE—brought up to date for version 1.1—uses tutorials and practical examples to build effective, and increasingly sophisticated, database management skills. Advanced topics include custom reporting, managing multiple databases, and designing custom applications.

Understanding Oracle
James T. Perry
Joseph G. Lateer
634pp. Ref. 534-4
A comprehensive guide to the Oracle database management system for administrators, users, and applications developers. Covers everything in Version 5 from database basics to multi-user systems, performance, and development tools including SQL*Forms, SQL*Report, and SQL*Calc. Includes Fast Track speed notes.

Understanding Professional File
Gerry Litton
463pp. Re. 669-3
Build practical data management skills in an orderly fashion with this complete step-by-step tutorial—from creating a simple database, to building customized business applications.

Understanding R:BASE
Alan Simpson
Karen Watterson
609pp. Ref. 503-4
This is the definitive R:BASE tutorial, for use with either OS/2 or DOS. Hands-on lessons cover every aspect of the software, from creating and using a database, to custom systems. Includes Fast Track speed notes.

Understanding SQL
Martin Gruber
400pp. Ref. 644-8
This comprehensive tutorial in Structured Query Language (SQL) is suitable for beginners, and for SQL users wishing to increase their skills. From basic principles to complex SQL applications, the text builds fluency and confidence using concise hands-on lessons and easy-to-follow examples.

Up & Running with Q&A
Ranier Bartel
140pp. Ref. 645-6
Obtain practical results with Q&A in the shortest possible time. Learn to design and program forms, use macros, format text, use utilities, and more. Or use the book to help you decide whether to purchase the program.

SPREADSHEETS AND INTEGRATED SOFTWARE

1-2-3 for Scientists and Engineers
William J. Orvis
341pp. Ref. 407-0
Fast, elegant solutions to common problems in science and engineering, using Lotus 1-2-3. Tables and plotting, curve fitting, statistics, derivatives, integrals and differentials, solving systems of equations, and more.

Frequently Used QEMM386.SYS Parameters

ADAPTERRAM	An adapter has RAM in the specified range.
ADAPTERROM	An adapter has ROM in the specified range.
AUTO	Turn on QEMM-386 only if necessary.
COMPAQ386S	Identify this as a Compaq 386S computer.
COMPAQEGAROM	Relocate a Compaq computer's video ROM.
COMPAQHALFROM	Split system ROM in half.
COMPAQROMMEMORY	Use Compaq memory reserved for ROM.
DISKBUF	Set the size of the SCSI disk buffer.
DMA	Set the size of the DMA buffer.
DOS4	Alter EMS page ordering for DOS 4.00 with the /X option.
EXCLUDE	Consider the range unmappable.
EXTMEM	Reserve the specified amount of extended memory.
FORCEEMS	Act like expanded memory.
FRAME	Set the beginning page frame address.
FRAMELENGTH	Set the frame's length.
HANDLES	Set the number of handles used to access memory.
HELP	Display a descriptive list of all QEMM-386 parameters.
INCLUDE	Consider the range mappable.
LOCKDMA	Don't use interrupts while processing DMA.
MAPS	Set the number of alternate maps available.